THE TEACHER CLARITY
PLAYBOOK

THE TEACHER CLARITY PLAYBOOK

A Hands-On Guide to Creating Learning Intentions and Success Criteria for Organized, Effective Instruction

Grades K–12

DOUGLAS FISHER
NANCY FREY
OLIVIA AMADOR
JOSEPH ASSOF

FOREWORD BY JOHN HATTIE

CORWIN
Fisher & Frey

FOR INFORMATION:

Corwin
A SAGE Company
2455 Teller Road
Thousand Oaks, California 91320
(800) 233-9936
www.corwin.com

SAGE Publications Ltd.
1 Oliver's Yard
55 City Road
London, EC1Y 1SP
United Kingdom

SAGE Publications India Pvt. Ltd.
B 1/I 1 Mohan Cooperative Industrial
Area
Mathura Road, New Delhi 110 044
India

SAGE Publications Asia-Pacific Pte. Ltd.
3 Church Street
#10-04 Samsung Hub
Singapore 049483

Director and Publisher, Corwin
Classroom: Lisa Luedeke
Editorial Development Manager: Julie Nemer
Senior Editorial Assistant: Sharon Wu
Production Editor: Laureen Gleason
Copy Editor: Amy Hanquist Harris
Typesetter: Integra
Proofreader: Gretchen Treadwell
Interior Designer: Scott Van Atta
Cover Designer and illustrator: Taryl Hansen

Printed Canada.

ISBN 978-1-5443-3981-8

This book is printed on acid-free paper.

18 19 20 21 22 10 9 8 7 6 5 4 3 2 1

CONTENTS

Visit the companion website at

resources.corwin.com/teacherclarityplaybook

for additional resources, including practice pages, video,

a Professional Learning Guide, and PowerPoint slides.

FOREWORD

By John Hattie

This book makes a bold claim. It describes excellent teachers as those who have appropriately high expectations; who share their notions of success criteria with their students; who ensure that there is constructive alignment between the lesson, the tasks, and the assignment; who ensure that the delivery of the lesson is relevant, accurate, and comprehensible to students; who give worked examples to illustrate the degree of cognitive complexity desired from their students; and who provide welcome feedback about where to move to next. This is what *teacher clarity* means throughout this book.

Consider the converse situation. I come into class as a student, and there are no expectations about how I will succeed. I do not know what success means (other than finishing my work by the bell); I do not see the relation between what my teacher is saying and asking me to do and what I do; I do not understand a lot of what my teacher says (but I pretend to listen, in case I get reprimanded); I know that I need to write something for the assignment or task, no matter what; and I know that whatever I do, the teacher will just ask me to do more. How many of these students do you have in your class? Now, consider *who* could make a difference to these students. This book shows *you* how to make that difference—and it also explains how students can help in this process. The joint aim is to turn students on to the excitement and joy of learning, while still instilling in them the notion that learning requires hard work.

The clarity claims in this book are underpinned by the notion of expertise. It takes expertise to appropriately diagnose the learning needs of all students relative to what they know, can do, and care about now; it takes expertise to devise optimal interventions and then ensure the fidelity of those interventions; and it takes expertise to evaluate the impact of each lesson on the student and how to modify the instruction (either during the current lesson or in the next lesson) in light of this impact. This impact involves not only what is intended to be known but also what needs to be comprehended; what is unknown; what is transferred to near and far tasks; what learning strategies are being used and whether there are other, more effective strategies that can be taught; and the depth or complexity of the learning as experienced by the student.

Consider the top eight ideals and corresponding effect sizes as described in the Visible Learning research: (1) Teachers and students, working together, evaluate their impact (d = .90); (2) all have high expectations (d = .90); (3) all move toward explicit success criteria (d = .77); (4) all use the Goldilocks principle of challenge (not too hard, not too boring; d = .74); (5) all see that errors and trust present opportunities to learn (d = .72); (6) all maximize feedback to themselves about their impact (d = .72); (7) all focus on enjoying learning and appreciate that learning involves hard work; and (8) all ensure that there is the optimal proportion of surface to deep learning (d = .69). Clarity is one of the more powerful causal mechanisms to ensure that these eight goals are reached. Clarity can provide evidence of the learning's relevance to the student, so that the learning is meaningful—and this book's two modules on relevance and making meaning are worth their weight in gold.

At the end of the book, there is a challenge: "Focusing on teacher clarity could revolutionize your practice." Enjoy the revolution—certainly, your students will.

LIST OF VIDEOS

Note From the Publisher: The authors have provided video and web content throughout the book that is available to you through QR (quick response) codes. To read a QR code, you must have a smartphone or tablet with a camera. We recommend that you download a QR code reader app that is made specifically for your phone or tablet brand.

Videos may also be accessed at **resources.corwin.com/teacherclarityplaybook**

Introduction Video

Module 1: Identifying Concepts and Skills

Video 1.1   Module 1 Overview

Video 1.2   Module 1 in Action—Elementary

Video 1.3   Module 1 in Action—Secondary

Module 2: Sequencing Learning Progressions

Video 2.1   Module 2 Overview

Video 2.2   Module 2 in Action—Elementary

Module 3: Elaborating Learning Intentions

Video 3.1   Module 3 Overview

Video 3.2   Module 3 in Action—Secondary

Module 4: Crafting Success Criteria

Video 4.1   Module 4 Overview

Video 4.2   Module 4 in Action—Elementary

Video 4.3   Module 4 in Action—Secondary

Module 5: Modifying Learning Intentions to Include Language Expectations

Video 5.1   Module 5 Overview

Video 5.2   Module 5 in Action—Elementary

Video 5.3   Module 5 in Action—Secondary

PUBLISHER'S ACKNOWLEDGMENTS

Corwin gratefully acknowledges the contributions of the following individuals:

Kris Allen
Classroom Teacher and Higher
   Education Faculty Member
Contoocook Valley School District
   and Western Governors University
Manchester, NH

John Almarode
Associate Professor
James Madison University
Harrisonburg, VA

Heather Anderson
Teacher/Teacher Leader
San Diego Unified School District
San Diego, CA

Annie Boulytchev
Teacher
Chula Vista Elementary School District
Chula Vista, CA

Ketti Davis
Assistant Superintendent/Chief
   Academic Officer
Central Unified School District
Fresno, CA

Linda Gomez
Teacher
Chula Vista Elementary School District
Chula Vista, CA

Hilda Martinez
RTI Literacy Coordinator
San Diego Unified School District
San Diego, CA

Brandi Sheppy
Resource Teacher
Chula Vista Elementary School District
Chula Vista, CA

Erika Tucker
K-12 Literacy Coordinator
Rockdale County Public Schools
Conyers, GA

Ashley Vasquez
Administrator
Chula Vista Elementary School District
Chula Vista, CA

INTRODUCTION

◄ **INTRODUCTION VIDEO**
resources.corwin.com/teacherclarityplaybook

To read a QR code, you must have a smartphone or tablet with a camera. We recommend that you download a QR code reader app that is made specifically for your phone or tablet brand.

Think about the last time you were engaged in learning something. Perhaps it was for work, perhaps not. When you think about all of the things that helped you learn, what stands out? Was it the intentional actions of a teacher and the opportunity to learn from other students? Was it the design of learning experiences? Was it the flow of those experiences? In reality, it was probably all of the above.

When Doug wanted to learn to use Final Cut Pro to edit videos, he didn't just practice with the software by himself, hoping he would get better. Instead, he attended seminars at the Apple store, engaged in online learning through Lynda .com, and joined a user's group to problem solve with others. In each case, there was a clear set of learning expectations and experiences that were designed to increase his understanding and ability to actually use the program. In each case, there was a clear path toward proficiency, with milestones identified along the way.

When learning is organized and intentional, and when the learner knows what he or she is learning, great things can happen. When students don't know what they are learning, don't care about their learning, and have no idea if they are learning, great things are unlikely to happen.

Enter *teacher clarity*. When teachers are clear in the expectations and instruction, students learn more. Fendick (1990) defined *teacher clarity* as "a measure of the clarity of communication between teachers and students in both directions" (p. 10) and further described it across four dimensions:

1. **Clarity of organization**, such that lesson tasks, assignments, and activities include links to the objectives and outcomes of learning.

2. **Clarity of explanation**, such that information is relevant, accurate, and comprehensible to students.

3. **Clarity of examples and guided practice**, such that the lesson includes information that is illustrative and illuminating as students gradually move to independence, making progress with less support from the teacher.

4. **Clarity of assessment of student learning**, such that the teacher is regularly seeking out and acting upon the feedback he or she receives from students, especially through their verbal and written responses.

As we noted earlier, when students know what they are learning and the lesson flows well, students learn more. Teacher clarity has an effect size of 0.75 (Hattie, 2009). Effect sizes are statistical measures that allow readers to determine how powerful a specific influence is on learning. John Hattie has assembled the largest educational research database in history and has calculated effect sizes on over 200 influences on learning. The average effect size in his database is 0.40. At 0.40, an effect is equal to approximately one year of learning for one year spent in school. Teacher clarity, with an effect size of 0.75, is likely to ensure that the impact on students is significantly greater than average. Of course, some students need to learn more than a year's worth of content to catch up. But at the minimum, students need to gain a year for a year. And teacher clarity can help.

A major part of teacher clarity is understanding what students need to learn and identifying how they will know that they learned it. To get there, teachers have to analyze standards and plan meaningful instruction and assessments. But planning should be focused on impact, not on instruction. Yes, teams of teachers can talk about how they will engage students in meaningful learning, but they must focus on the impact of those activities on learning. In doing so, they clarify their expectations. And expectations also have a powerful impact on students' learning.

TEACHER EXPECTATIONS

Teacher expectations have a powerful influence on student achievement, with an effect size of 0.43 (Hattie, 2009). In large part, teachers get what they expect; teachers with low expectations are particularly successful at getting what they expect. Teacher expectations for students vary by race, ethnicity, and socioeconomic status. However, these can be disrupted by focusing on specific strategies for resetting expectations. These strategies include linking teaching goals to uniformly high standards, flexible and responsive teaching, and assessment that informs both students and teachers (Rubie-Davies & Rosenthal, 2016).

Establishing and communicating learning intentions is an important way that teachers share their expectations with students. When these learning intentions are compared with grade-level expectations or expectations in other schools and districts, educators can get a sense of their appropriateness (and the expectations they have for students). Analyzing the success criteria is another way of determining the expectations a teacher has for students. A given learning intention could have multiple success criteria, some of which may be at the surface level of learning and others of which may at deeper levels of learning. The success criteria communicate the level of performance that students are expected to meet and allow teams of teachers to talk about the learning expected of students.

In addition, the experiences that teachers plan and the assessments they use also communicate the expectations that they have for students. Teachers with low expectations tend to talk a lot to students (averaging about 80% of the minutes each week) and assess students at the basic skill level. Teachers with higher expectations tend to talk less (averaging about 50% of the minutes each week) and assess students at deeper levels of understanding.

Each of these (learning intentions, success criteria, meaningful experiences, and assessments) are components of teacher clarity, and each can be used to foster students learning.

LEARNING INTENTIONS AND SUCCESS CRITERIA CONTRIBUTE TO TEACHER CLARITY

A major aspect of teacher clarity consists of learning intentions and success critiera. The evidence on the effectiveness of learning intentions and success criteria is impressive. Hattie and Donoghue (2016) examined 31 meta-analyses of more than 3,300 studies related to success criteria and reported an overall effect size of 0.54. When students know what success looks like, they are more likely to plan and predict, set goals, and acquire a stronger sense of how to judge their own progress. In other words, they recognize that they have something to learn and what it looks like when they have learned it.

The content standards for a grade level and discipline shape the expectations held in common for a state's or territory's students. Careful analysis of content standards benefits those who need to teach them—the educators themselves. Through the process of discussion and debate, colleagues identify what students should know and be able to do, and thus prevent the inevitable "creep" that occurs when textbooks and activities, not the standards, begin to drive instruction. Keep in mind that publisher- and teacher-created curricula are not the standards themselves, but rather are materials that (hopefully) facilitate progress toward standards. But when discussions at a grade-level meeting are focused more on covering a chapter in a textbook rather than the learning outcomes, it is a telltale sign that the standard has been lost.

TEACHER COLLABORATION IS VITAL FOR RAISING EXPECTATIONS

The best way to improve teacher clarity is to do so in the company of others. You may be using this playbook as a team. In that case, you probably have collaboration baked into your professional learning processes. One common structure for fostering teacher collaboration to improve the quality of learning has been the formation of professional learning communities (PLCs). PLCs usually involve small groups of educators who have come together to support each other's learning for the purpose of improving student achievement. These are not book clubs or professional learning sessions. The use of these five PLC+ questions keeps the focus relentlessly on the learning outcomes of students and explains why the impact of PLCs is powerful (Fisher et al., 2019):

- Where are we going?

- Where are we now?

- How do we move learning forward?

- What did we learn today?

- Who benefited and who did not?

These discussions can result in improved instruction as well as better outcomes for students (e.g., Lai, Wilson, McNaughton, & Hsiao, 2014). In collaborative teams, teachers identify learning intentions and discuss ideas for instruction. They meet to review student work and figure out if their efforts have been fruitful. They also talk about students who need additional instruction or intervention to be successful.

Each of these five questions is answered as teams engage in teacher clarity work. Figure 1 provides an overview of the modules of teacher clarity linked with the PLC+ questions. Although we have presented a sequence of modules, teams typically talk about all five questions in an integrated way.

FIGURE 1 PLC+ Questions and Teacher Clarity

PLC+ Question	Teacher Clarity Module	Description
Where are we going?	- Module 1: Identifying Concepts and Skills - Module 2: Sequencing Learning Progressions - Module 3: Elaborating Learning Intentions - Module 4: Crafting Success Criteria	In these modules, teachers or teams of teachers are analyzing the standards to determine what students need to know. They are sequencing learning such that it is logical and allows for both content and language to develop.
Where are we now?	- Module 5: Modifying Learning Intentions to Include Language Expectations - Module 6: Determining the Relevance of the Learning	In these modules, teachers identify the relevance of the learning expectations to ensure that students are engaged and motivated and consider any additional language needs.
How do we move learning forward?	- Module 7: Designing Assessment Opportunities - Module 8: Creating Meaningful Learning Experiences	Teachers design formative assessment experiences to monitor progress, aligned with meaningful learning experiences.
What did we learn today? Who benefited and who did not?	- Module 9: Establishing Mastery of Standards	Teachers identify summative assessment tools that can be used to determine mastery of the standards, and to monitor progress through instruction and intervention.

Meaningful teacher collaboration builds collective teacher efficacy, which is a constellation of attitudes and beliefs about the efforts of a school to affect student learning (Goddard, Hoy, & Hoy, 2000). More to the point, teachers with a high collective efficacy believe that "teachers in this school can get through to the most difficult students" (p. 480). Importantly, perceptions are based on experiences. When teachers experience success collaborating with peers and those collaborations improve teaching and learning, they notice. These accumulated data points become the collective efficacy that researchers note is so powerful. With an effect size of 1.57, collective teacher efficacy is number one on Hattie's list of influences on student achievement, more than tripling the speed of learning.

USING THIS PLAYBOOK

It is great if you are able to use this playbook as part of your collaboration with other educators, but you might be using this playbook on your own. In that case, never fear! We hope that we have been able to create a tool that allows for dialogue to occur between us. In the back of the book and on the companion website for this book (resources.corwin.com/teacherclarityplaybook), you will find *sample* answers for the guided-practice phase of each step in the process. These are not absolutes, but rather are representative of our thinking as we worked with experienced elementary and secondary teachers to develop these examples. You may have answers that differ from the ones we furnished; all we ask is that you are able to justify your responses in ways that are consistent with high expectations for student learning. In turn, we hope that you will remain open to our responses. After all, reading is about engaging in silent dialogue with the author.

THE MODULES

Each of the nine learning modules in this notebook is designed to move you systematically through a process that begins and ends with the standards, from analysis through assessment. Our intent is not to introduce you to a process that you must implement in a lockstep way, but rather to build a habit of mind for how it is that you systematically and efficiently analyze standards, build curriculum, teach, and assess. In other words, this process can mobilize the impact of teacher clarity in your classroom. A flowchart for the nine modules can be found in Figure 2.

THE LEARNING PROCESS

Each module uses a modified version of the gradual release of responsibility instructional framework (Fisher & Frey, 2014). Each begins with an explanation of the core concepts of the module to establish the purpose for learning and provide

FIGURE 2

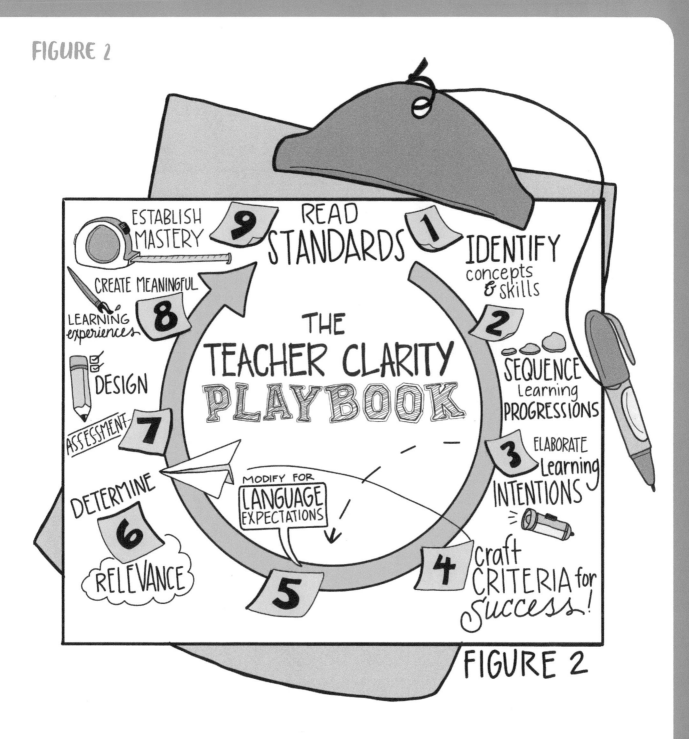

FIGURE 2

direct explanation. The module then continues with modeling how the process is applied through four examples:

- First-grade math

- Fourth-grade English language arts

- Eighth-grade algebra

- Tenth-grade English language arts

We integrate examples from the Next Generation Science Standards and from social studies standards in the Guided Practice sections. We focus on a single standard for ease in explanation, knowing that many teachers plan lessons that address multiple standards at the same time. Thankfully, the process is the same but a little more complicated.

Although some will resonate more with you than others, depending on your own professional interests, we encourage you to engage with all the examples so you can see a pattern across grade and content areas.

Guided practice comes next, and the content and grade levels vary across modules. The Guided Practice section is for you to write on and discuss with your team, if possible. We have suggested answers in the back of the book to help you, but, as noted earlier, they should not be interpreted too narrowly as the *only* correct response. Each module ends with an Independent Practice section in which you apply the same process to a grade level and subject area you have selected. Although it is independent learning, we hope you will be able to continue discussion with colleagues.

OUR HOPE

We really do believe that teacher clarity is important—critical, even. In fact, we believe that it is key to the Visible Learning story (Hattie, 2012). We don't promise that it is easy work or that you will have the time to do this for every lesson, but we do promise that if you see this through to the classroom, you will detect a notable positive change in how you and your students talk about learning. What could be better than that?

NOTES

NOTES

_____

_____

_____

_____

_____

_____

_____

_____

_____

_____

_____

_____

_____

_____

_____

_____

_____

_____

_____

_____

_____

_____

_____

_____

_____

MODULE 1: IDENTIFYING CONCEPTS AND SKILLS

◀ VIDEO 1.1 Module 1 Overview
resources.corwin.com/teacherclarityplaybook

A simple glance through a standards document is not sufficient to teach those standards. Knowing the standards well allows teachers to identify the necessary prior knowledge and to determine the expectations for students' success. In nearly all cases, the standards themselves articulate outcomes of learning and often call upon students to apply what they have learned to an ever-widening set of situations and texts. These outcome standards can't be mastered in a day or a week. They require intentional instruction that is sustained over many lessons and learning experiences.

WHAT CONTENT KNOWLEDGE DO STUDENTS NEED TO BE SUCCESSFUL?

A useful method for determining the concepts students must master and the skills they need to attain is to analyze the standard's nouns and verbs. The nouns in a standard generally represent what it is the student needs to know—the concepts. This is the core knowledge of the discipline, and it encompasses the following:

- *Declarative knowledge,* which is the factual information associated with the subject.

- *Procedural knowledge,* which is the application of information.

- *Conditional knowledge,* which is knowing when the information should be used.

Many of the nouns in a standard reveal the declarative, procedural, and/or conditional knowledge the student needs to learn. Another way of saying this is that these are the content demands. Take this example from the Michigan Social Studies Standards for Grade 8, with key nouns and noun phrases identified:

STANDARD(S)	
Develop an argument based on <u>evidence</u> about the positive and negative <u>consequences of territorial</u> and <u>economic expansion</u> on <u>Native Americans.</u>	
CONCEPTS (NOUNS)	**SKILLS (VERBS)**
Evidence Consequences of territorial expansion Consequences of economic expansion Native Americans	

We didn't underline *positive* and *negative* in this case because we wanted to focus for now on the essential nouns. That is not to say that these adjectives are not important. Quite to the contrary, they are because they provide further detail and nuance about the concepts that need to be taught. But for now, we just want to tease out the key nouns present.

Also note that we just presented one standard. In many subject areas, teachers are actually teaching multiple standards at the same time. In that case, you'd list all of the standards in the top box, identify the range of concepts (nouns) and later skills (verbs), and then continue the process outlined in this playbook.

WHAT SKILLS MUST STUDENTS DEMONSTRATE TO BE SUCCESSFUL?

Of course, teaching is far more than just pouring facts into the heads of students. Knowledge is more useful when it can be applied. The syntax of the standards helps us again, this time in the form of verbs. Many of the verbs in a standard speak to the skills students must acquire in order to make the concepts, and content, useful. Let's look again at the same standard, this time with the verbs underlined:

STANDARD(S)

<u>Develop an argument</u> based on evidence about the positive and negative consequences of territorial and economic expansion on American Indians.

CONCEPTS (NOUNS)	SKILLS (VERBS)
Evidence	Develop an
Consequences	argument
of territorial	
expansion	
Consequences	
of economic	
expansion	
Native Americans	

Chances are good that the moment you considered this verb phrase, you immediately began thinking in two divergent directions:

1. What other knowledge and skills would students need in order to develop such an argument?

2. How might a student demonstrate this skill?

The first question speaks to the prior knowledge and skills needed, while the second question addresses wonderings about teaching and assessment. That's understandable, but we'd like for you to hold those wonderings for the time being. Rather, let's consider what the term *develop* signals. It suggests that students are constructing knowledge, not simply reproducing facts, which requires them to use declarative, procedural, and conditional knowledge. These are the skills that students must apply to the concepts. It is equally important to recognize what the word *develop* doesn't say. Nowhere is there a directive about how it will be accomplished or what it will look like. The outcome might occur in an argumentative essay, a presentation, or a debate. Those decisions are yet to come as you analyze for learning progressions, learning intentions, and success criteria in the coming modules.

PLC CONVERSATIONS

1. **What challenged you in this module?**

2. **How will you package and pace the standards? Would a pacing guide for all of the standards be useful?**

3. **How will you know if you analyzed the standard(s) correctly?**

MODELING

Here are modeled examples of standards with the nouns and verbs identified.

STANDARD(S)

Solve word problems that call for addition of three whole numbers whose sum is less than or equal to 20 (e.g., by using objects, drawings, and equations with a symbol for the unknown number to represent the problem).

CONCEPTS (NOUNS)	SKILLS (VERBS)
Word problem	Solve
Addition	Use
Whole numbers	Represent
Sum	
Objects	
Drawings	
Equations	
Symbol	
Unknown number	
Problem	

GRADE 4: ENGLISH LANGUAGE ARTS (ELA)

STANDARD(S)

Determine the main idea of a text and explain how it is supported by key details; summarize the text.

CONCEPTS (NOUNS)	SKILLS (VERBS)
Main idea	Determine
Key details	Explain
Text	Summarize

GRADE 8: ALGEBRA

STANDARD(S)

Know and apply the properties of integer exponents to generate equivalent numerical expressions.

CONCEPTS (NOUNS)	SKILLS (VERBS)
Properties of integer exponents	Know
Equivalent numerical expressions	Apply
	Generate

GRADE 10: ENGLISH

STANDARD(S)

Cite strong and thorough textual evidence to support analysis of what the text says explicitly as well as inferences drawn from the text.

CONCEPTS (NOUNS)	SKILLS (VERBS)
Textual evidence	Cite
Analysis of explicit text	Support
Analysis of inferences	Draw from

GUIDED PRACTICE

For the following examples, identify the nouns and verbs. First, underline them; then, place them in the corresponding boxes.

GRADE 7: ELA

STANDARD(S)

Write arguments to support claims with clear reasons and relevant evidence. (c) Use words, phrases, and clauses to create cohesion and clarify the relationships among claim(s), reasons, and evidence.

CONCEPTS (NOUNS)	SKILLS (VERBS)

GRADE 3: MATH (FLORIDA)

STANDARD(S)

Tell and write time to the nearest minute and measure time intervals in minutes. Solve word problems involving addition and subtraction of time intervals in minutes—for example, by representing the problem on a number line diagram.

CONCEPTS (NOUNS)	SKILLS (VERBS)

Note: For suggested answers, please turn to page 123 or visit the companion website at **resources.corwin.com/teacherclarityplaybook**.

INDEPENDENT PRACTICE

Fill in your own standards in the following boxes; then, identify the nouns and verbs as you did in the Guided Practice section.

STANDARD(S)

CONCEPTS (NOUNS)

SKILLS (VERBS)

STANDARD(S)

CONCEPTS (NOUNS)

SKILLS (VERBS)

WATCH!

Videos and viewing guide may also be accessed at **resources.corwin.com/teacherclarityplaybook**

VIDEO 1.2
Module 1 in Action—Elementary
resources.corwin.com/teacherclarityplaybook

VIDEO 1.3
Module 1 in Action—Secondary
resources.corwin.com/teacherclarityplaybook

NOTES

_____

_____

_____

_____

_____

_____

_____

_____

_____

_____

_____

_____

_____

_____

_____

_____

_____

_____

MODULE 2: SEQUENCING LEARNING PROGRESSIONS

◀ VIDEO 2.1 Module 2 Overview
resources.corwin.com/teacherclarityplaybook

Standards can't be learned in a single day. Instead, they represent the knowledge gained through extended experience and interaction with the content. Identifying the concepts and skills within a standard, or groups of standards, reveals information in the form of the concepts and skills to be learned, but also, as noted in Module 1, raises other questions.

- First, what underlying prior knowledge must students possess?

- Second, how might the concepts and skills within this standard be sequenced in a logical way?

A sequence of learning progressions frames the planning needed for students to reliably learn. This marks a process some call "unpacking" or "unwrapping" the standards. We rely on backwards planning that begins with the outcome standard and the ways in which students will demonstrate mastery of that standard—in other words, how the teacher will assess the learning. We have included mastery of standards as the last module in this playbook to demonstrate the flow of the lesson, but some teams turn to that section now and focus on the ways in which students will demonstrate their learning.

Of course, the planning process also includes a range of meaningful experiences that guide students toward mastery as teachers check for understanding along the learning journey, making modifications based on how quickly students are grasping the information. We have focused on the meaningful learning experiences that teachers design in Module 8. This module focuses on the logical progression of learning.

Learning progressions articulate a pathway to proficiency. The learning progressions are like tent poles for a unit of study in that they delineate the major supports for the standard. To use another metaphor, they are the stones that mark a path. Standards provide the scope and sequence of a curricular area that show how concepts are broadly developed from kindergarten through high school. Learning progressions are more fine-grained and describe the intermediate steps students will use to reach mastery.

Learning progressions differ from learning intentions, which we will address in the next module. Learning intentions expand each of the learning progressions into daily statements of expectations for students. But it is too broad a leap to move directly from a standard to the daily learning intentions. The learning progressions aid in setting forth a path that will lead to the desired outcome standard. Learning progressions are the essential core concepts and processes that underlie the standard (and they can be used to design assessments of mastery, as we will see in Module 7).

DETERMINING A LEARNING PROGRESSION

We will use a middle school Next Generation Science Standard (NGSS) to demonstrate the process of developing a learning progression. Once the concepts (nouns) and skills (verbs) have been identified, the next step is to analyze the logical progress of learning. Let's consider the following standard:

MS-LS1-1. Conduct an investigation to provide evidence that living things are made of cells—either one cell or many different numbers and types of cells.

To gain mastery on this standard, students need to develop an understanding of the presence of cells as a condition for being a living thing, as well as the ability to carry out an investigation that will illustrate the core disciplinary concept. In addition, students need to be knowledgeable about gathering and reporting evidence when conducting an investigation, and they need to understand that living things are composed of cells. Therefore, a possible approach for this standard might be to have five learning progressions, each with some number of learning intentions. Each of them would start with "I am learning about . . ."

1. the differences between living and nonliving things.

2. the characteristics of unicellular and multicellular living things.

3. using a microscope and related scientific equipment to identify cell types.

4. data gathered from a cell investigation and how to extract and analyze data.

5. arguments supported by evidence to support or refute the claim that living things are composed of cells.

These are not individual lessons, and some may in fact involve previously mastered skills (e.g., using a microscope). However, identifying a progression for learning ensures that students consolidate concepts and skills in a coherent and cohesive manner. Once these learning progressions have been identified, each can be further expanded into daily learning intentions, which will be addressed in the next module. See Figure 3 for a visual representation of the relationship.

Importantly, there is no right number of learning progressions (or learning intentions). As we metaphorically noted earlier, these are the tent poles, and we recommend that there are enough of them to support students' learning. Remember that the learning progressions are broader statements from which the daily learning intentions are developed.

Based on the students in your class, some of the individual learning progressions may have already been mastered. For example, the middle school students might already know how to use a microscope, so the teacher could skip that one, even though it might be important for students in another class to focus on. In other words, learning progressions detail the logical order of students' learning, and teachers decide where to start and what to include, based on their knowledge of their students.

FIGURE 3 **The Relationship Between Learning Progressions and Learning Intentions**

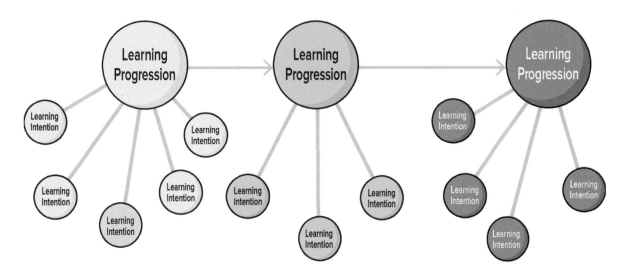

In some cases, there are sample learning progressions provided for teachers, such as the following:

- Progressions Documents for the Common Core Math Standards: ime.math.arizona.edu/progressions

- Learning Trajectories for the K–8 Common Core Math Standards: www.turnonccmath.net

- ELA Learning Progressions (Delaware Department of Education): www.doe.k12.de.us/Page/2036

- A discussion about learning progressions in science can be found at http://www.sensepublishers.com/media/593-learning-progressions-in-science.pdf

- A list of learning progressions in social studies can be found at http://www.lewiscentral.org/departments/curriculum__instruction/curriculum_framework_and_standards/content_areas/social_studies/k-12_learning_progressions_in_social_studies/

PLC CONVERSATIONS

1. What challenged you in this module?

2. How are learning progressions different from learning intentions, and why is this important?

3. How can you reach agreement about the learning progressions for a given standard?

NOTES

_____

_____

_____

_____

_____

_____

_____

_____

_____

_____

MODELING

The following are examples of standards and **learning progressions** for the ELA and math standards we analyzed in Module 1.

GRADE 1: MATH

STANDARD(S)

Solve word problems that call for addition of three whole numbers whose sum is less than or equal to 20 (e.g., by using objects, drawings, and equations with a symbol for the unknown number to represent the problem).

CONCEPTS (NOUNS)

Word problem
Addition
Whole numbers
Sum
Objects
Drawings
Equations
Symbol
Unknown number
Problem

SKILLS (VERBS)

Solve
Use
Represent

LEARNING PROGRESSION

1. Analyze word problems to determine which actions and attributes call for the operation of addition.

2. Analyze word problems to identify whole numbers in the task.

3. Use objects to represent numbers in a word problem and add those objects together.

4. Use drawings to represent numbers in a word problem and add those objects together.

5. Develop an equation to represent the information in the word problem.

6. Use a symbol to represent the unknown number in a word problem.

7. Solve problems that contain three addends in a word problem.

GRADE 4: ELA

STANDARD(S)

Determine the main idea of a text and explain how it is supported by key details; summarize the text.

CONCEPTS (NOUNS)	SKILLS (VERBS)
Main idea	Determine
Key details	Explain
Text	Summarize

LEARNING PROGRESSION

1. Identify at least three details in an informational text.

2. Recognize the central or main idea when the author provides a topic sentence.

3. Determine the central or main idea when the author does not provide a topic sentence.

4. Using the main idea and details, summarize the information provided in the text.

5. Explain how the details in a text support the central or main idea.

GRADE 8: ALGEBRA

STANDARD(S)

Know and apply the properties of integer exponents to generate equivalent numerical expressions.

CONCEPTS (NOUNS)	SKILLS (VERBS)
Properties of integer exponents	Know
Equivalent numerical expressions	Apply
	Generate

LEARNING PROGRESSION

1. Discover and use the product and quotient properties of exponents.

2. Discover and use the meaning of an exponent of 0.

3. Define negative exponents and use them to rewrite exponential expressions.

4. Discover and use the power to a power property of exponents.

5. Generate equivalent expressions by applying multiple properties of exponents.

GRADE 10: ENGLISH

STANDARD(S)

Cite strong and thorough textual evidence to support analysis of what the text says explicitly as well as inferences drawn from the text.

CONCEPTS (NOUNS)

Textual evidence

Analysis of explicit text

Analysis of inferences

SKILLS (VERBS)

Cite

Support analysis

Draw from

LEARNING PROGRESSION

1. Determine the major themes, plot, characters, and setting of the text.

2. Make inferences about the text.

3. Create a logical claim based on the text.

4. Use evidence to support an analysis of what the text explicitly says.

5. Use evidence to support inferences drawn from the text.

6. Use formal reasoning to explain how the evidence supports your claim.

7. Use MLA format for citations.

GUIDED PRACTICE

We have written learning progressions for the following eighth-grade social studies standard. For your first task, place the learning progressions in a logical sequence. Put 1 next to the one you believe comes first, 2 on the next logical progression, and so on.

Ohio Social Studies Standard 21
Grade 8: Roles and Systems of Government
The U.S. Constitution protects citizens' rights by limiting the powers of government.

___ Describe the role of the U.S. Constitution as a foundational document.

___ Identify the three branches of the U.S. government.

___ Explain what is meant by the "powers of the government."

___ Understand the conflict of the framers in balancing states' rights with federal government powers.

___ Recognize the Bill of Rights' role in limiting the powers of government.

___ Enumerate the protections provided to U.S. citizens by the Constitution as amended.

For this second task, create a set of learning progressions for the following standard for students in first-grade ELA:

Distinguish shades of meaning among verbs differing in manner (e.g., look, peek, glance, stare, glare, scowl) and adjectives differing in intensity (e.g., large, gigantic, small, tiny) by defining or choosing them or by acting out the meanings.

1. _____

2. _____

3. _____

4. _____

5. _____

6. _____

7. _____

8. _____

Note: For suggested answers, please turn to page 124 or visit the companion website at **resources.corwin.com/teacherclarityplaybook.**

INDEPENDENT PRACTICE

Now, practice on your own. Fill in your own standards, identify nouns and verbs, and write learning progressions that follow a logical sequence.

STANDARD(S)

CONCEPTS (NOUNS)   SKILLS (VERBS)

LEARNING PROGRESSION

1.

2.

3.

4.

5.

6.

7.

8.

WATCH!

Videos and viewing guide may also be accessed at **resources.corwin.com/teacherclarityplaybook**

VIDEO 2.2
Module 2 in Action—Elementary
resources.corwin.com/teacherclarityplaybook

NOTES

_____

_____

_____

_____

_____

_____

_____

_____

_____

_____

_____

_____

_____

_____

_____

_____

_____

_____

MODULE 3: ELABORATING LEARNING INTENTIONS

◄ VIDEO 3.1 Module 3 Overview
resources.corwin.com/teacherclarityplaybook

Standards are statements for teachers that identify what students should know and be able to do at a given point in time. Standards are too broad for students to master in a single lesson. And, as a matter of fact, some standards might need to be addressed over the span of multiple units of study. Effective teachers start with a standard to identify the content and skills. They then identify the learning progressions that are required to meet the standard. You have already practiced doing both.

Next, they break the learning progressions extracted from that standard into lesson-sized chunks and phrase these chunks so that students will be able to understand them. Each one of these chunked phrases—a daily statement of what a student is expected to learn in a given lesson—is a *learning intention*.

Learning intentions can focus on knowledge, skills, or concepts. Here are a few examples of learning intentions:

1. I am learning about the impact of the setting on a character.
2. I am learning about rotation of the sun and moon.
3. I am learning about the persuasive techniques used in advertising.

Figure 4 provides less- and more-effective examples of learning intentions. Note that one difference is that the task is emphasized in the less-effective examples, whereas the learning is emphasized in the more-effective examples.

Learning intentions have a priming effect on learners. They signal to the students what they will be learning or what they have learned. For example, students need to understand that a particular math activity is for the purpose of building fluency or that the assigned reading in science is to build the background knowledge they'll need for the lab experiment they'll soon be completing.

FIGURE 4 Less- and More-Effective Learning Intentions

LESS EFFECTIVE	CONTENT AREA	MORE EFFECTIVE
Draw a map with land and water identified.	**Kindergarten history / social studies**	I am learning how land and water are represented on maps and globes.
Analyze your writing using the checklist for task, purpose, and audience.	**Grade 4 English language arts**	I am learning about the role that author's purpose and audience play in my writing.
Complete questions 9–15 in Chapter 6.	**Middle school math**	I am learning about the relationship between rational numbers, decimals, and long division.
Explain Newton's Third Law.	**High school science**	I am learning that forces are composed of both a magnitude and direction.

COMMUNICATING LEARNING INTENTIONS

Learning intentions should be communicated in ways that are developmentally appropriate for the students you are teaching. After all, the benefits of establishing the goals for learning in the lesson will be completely lost if the learner can't understand them. Using the learning intentions listed earlier, we have further expanded them into student-friendly language:

1. Today, we'll read two stories about city and country life. We'll focus on comparing the lives of these two characters and the differences in their lives based on where they live. We'll figure out how the setting in these books where they live impacts them. When asked what they are learning, students would likely answer, "We are learning about setting and how that impacts characters."

2. As we revise our opinion papers, we are going to learn how to update our word choices so that we use technical vocabulary such as the authors we've been studying use. When asked what they are learning, students would likely answer, "We are learning about technical vocabulary in our writing."

3. As we have been learning, there are a number of techniques advertisers use, such as repetition, bandwagons, glittering generalities, and celebrity associations. Today, we'll look for examples of those in television ads. When asked what they are learning, students would likely answer, "We are learning about the techniques of advertisers."

TIMING LEARNING INTENTIONS

Some teachers might be concerned that statements such as these can rob students of a period of investigation and inquiry, but they can be written in a manner that doesn't give away the punchline, or they can be written with the investigation explicitly called out—"Discover the product property of exponents by expanding and simplifying exponential expressions."

Learning intentions don't have to be used exclusively at the outset of the lesson and, in fact, should be revisited over the course of the lesson. Teachers can withhold their learning intentions until after an exploration or discovery has occurred. And teachers can invite students to explain what they learned from the lesson and compare that with the initially stated learning intention for the lesson. Interesting class discussions about the alignment (or lack of alignment) can provide a great deal of insight on student understanding.

Having said that, we believe that daily learning intentions contribute to student success and efforts to ensure equity and excellence for students. When students do not know what they are expected to learn, the chance that they actually learn is reduced. There is even evidence that indicates when students know what they are supposed to be learning, they are three times more likely to learn it (Hattie, 2012).

PLC CONVERSATIONS

1. What challenged you in this module?

2. Do any of our learning intentions focus more on tasks than expectations for learning?

3. What language should we use so students in our grade understand the learning intentions?

MODELING

In the following four examples, you will find learning intentions based on one of the previously identified specific learning progressions.

GRADE 1: MATH

STANDARD(S)

Solve word problems that call for addition of three whole numbers whose sum is less than or equal to 20 (e.g., by using objects, drawings, and equations with a symbol for the unknown number to represent the problem).

CONCEPTS (NOUNS)	SKILLS (VERBS)
Word problem	Solve
Addition	Use
Whole numbers	Represent
Sum	
Objects	
Drawings	
Equations	
Symbol	
Unknown number	
Problem	

LEARNING PROGRESSION

5. Develop an equation to represent the information in the word problem.

LEARNING INTENTIONS

1. I am learning about number sentences.

2. I am learning to write number sentences based on models and pictures.

3. I am learning to look for errors in number sentences.

GRADE 4: ELA

STANDARD(S)

Determine the main idea of a text and explain how it is supported by key details; summarize the text.

CONCEPTS (NOUNS)	SKILLS (VERBS)
Main idea	Determine
Key details	Explain
Text	Summarize

LEARNING PROGRESSION

3. Determine the central or main idea when the author does not provide a topic sentence.

LEARNING INTENTIONS

1. I am learning about the concept of *main idea*.

2. I am learning about the differences between ideas and details presented in a text.

3. I am learning about the main idea of text and its importance in the organization of the text.

GRADE 8: ALGEBRA

STANDARD(S)

Know and apply the properties of integer exponents to generate equivalent numerical expressions.

CONCEPTS (NOUNS)	SKILLS (VERBS)
Properties of integer exponents	Know
Equivalent numerical expressions	Apply
	Generate

LEARNING PROGRESSION

1. Discover and use the product and quotient properties of exponents.

LEARNING INTENTIONS

1. I am learning how to discover the product property of exponents by expanding and simplifying exponential expressions.

2. I am learning how to apply the product property of exponents to solve problems.

3. I am learning how to discover the quotient property of exponents by expanding and simplifying exponential expressions.

4. I am learning how to apply the quotient property of exponents to solve problems.

GRADE 10: ENGLISH

STANDARD(S)

Cite strong and thorough textual evidence to support analysis of what the text says explicitly as well as inferences drawn from the text.

CONCEPTS (NOUNS)	SKILLS (VERBS)
Textual evidence	Cite
Analysis of explicit text	Support
Analysis of inferences	Draw from

LEARNING PROGRESSION

4. Use evidence to support an analysis of what the text explicitly says.

LEARNING INTENTIONS

1. I am learning about important details in the text.

2. I am learning about using evidence from a text to support my claim.

3. I am learning about inferences and the evidence I use to support them.

GUIDED PRACTICE

First, identify a logical sequence of **learning intentions** based on the learning progression and standard that follow:

Earth and Space Science (NGSS) HS-ESS2-1 Earth's Systems, Plate Tectonics and Large-Scale

Standard: *System Interactions:*
Plate tectonics is the unifying theory that explains the past and current movements of rocks at Earth's surface and provides a framework for understanding its geologic history.

One in a sequence of learning progressions:
3) There are three types of plate boundaries: subduction zones, divergent margins, and transform margins. Their movement results in various geological features and events.

Number these learning intentions in a logical sequence:

___ I am learning about the unique movements associated with the three types of plate boundaries.

___ I am learning about the differences between the types of geological features that result from plate boundaries' movement (subduction, divergent, and transform).

___ I am learning about geologic features that result from plate boundaries' movement.

___ I am learning about the characteristics of subduction zones, divergent zones, and transform margins.

___ I am learning the relationship between specific plate boundaries and geologic features.

For Part 2 of this practice, write a series of learning intentions based on the standard and the learning progression presented. Remember, there will be many more steps in the learning progression.

CONTINUED

CONTINUED

STANDARD(S)

Students understand the rule-making process in a direct democracy (everyone votes on the rules) and in a representative democracy (an elected group of people make the rules), giving examples of both systems in their classroom, school, and community. (Grade 1, CA Social Studies)

CONCEPTS (NOUNS)

Rule-making
Direct democracy
Representative democracy
Key details

SKILLS (VERBS)

Understand
Explain
Give examples

LEARNING PROGRESSION

3. Compare and contrast direct and representative democracy.

LEARNING INTENTIONS

1. _____

2. _____

3. _____

4. _____

5. _____

6. _____

7. _____

8. _____

Note: For suggested answers, please turn to page 125 or visit the companion website at **resources.corwin.com/teacherclarityplaybook**.

INDEPENDENT PRACTICE

For your independent practice, complete the template that follows with one of your standards and its concepts, skills, learning progressions, and learning intentions.

STANDARD(S)

CONCEPTS (NOUNS)   SKILLS (VERBS)

LEARNING PROGRESSION

LEARNING INTENTIONS

1.

2.

3.

4.

5.

6.

7.

8.

WATCH!

Videos and viewing guide may also be accessed at **resources.corwin.com/ teacherclarityplaybook**

VIDEO 3.2
Module 3 in Action—Secondary
resources.corwin.com/teacherclarityplaybook

NOTES

_____

_____

_____

_____

_____

_____

_____

_____

_____

_____

_____

_____

_____

_____

_____

_____

_____

_____

_____

MODULE 4: CRAFTING SUCCESS CRITERIA

◄ VIDEO 4.1 Module 4 Overview
resources.corwin.com/teacherclarityplaybook

How do you know whether your students are successful at learning what you wanted them to learn? How do *they* know whether they're successful? How can students know whether or not they've achieved the intended learning or whether they're making progress toward doing so? The daily learning intentions that are communicated by the teacher are an end product of careful planning. The success criteria provide a means for students and the teacher to gauge progress toward learning, thereby making learning visible to the teacher and the student.

Success criteria let students in on the secret that has been too often kept from them—what the destination looks like. Imagine getting into an airplane that was being flown by a pilot who didn't know where he or she was headed. Rather, a control tower would contact her at some unspecified time in the future to let her know she had arrived—or worse, that she missed the mark entirely. That is a completely irrational way to fly a plane. Yet students often have a similar experience. They're flying their own learning plane but have little sense of where they are headed. Wouldn't the trip be completed more successfully and efficiently if the pilot knew from the beginning where she or he was going?

Now imagine how much more successful and efficient learning would be if we enlisted students in their learning journeys. Success criteria signal the learner about the destination and provide a map for how they will get there.

Further, the success criteria empower learners to assess their own progress and not to be solely dependent on an outside agent (their teacher) to notice when they have arrived.

THE EFFECTIVENESS OF SUCCESS CRITERIA

Success criteria have been shown to increase students' internal motivation. And all of us have students who are not motivated—well, not motivated to learn *our* content. Success criteria (and relevance, as we will explore later) provide students with clear, specific, and attainable goals and can spark motivation in some of the most reluctant learners. A very convincing case could be made that internal motivation to succeed is one of the more important things your students can learn. Success criteria work because they tap into principles of human motivation. People tend to compare their current performance or ability to a goal that they have set or that a caring teacher has set with them. When there is a gap between where they are and where they want to be, cognitive dissonance is created, or as Piaget called it, *disequilibrium*. Students are motivated to close the gap and get rid of the dissonance by working and learning, and thus assimilating or accommodating information and ideas. The more explicitly and precisely they can see the goal, the more motivated they will likely be.

TYPES OF SUCCESS CRITERIA

Criteria such as "Do your best" and "Try hard" are not very clear or actionable. It may well be worthwhile to ban these phrases from your vocabulary, as they set very low targets. (Whatever the student does is often claimed as his best, yet this "best effort" may not be good enough.)

- Sometimes, teachers use "I can" statements that focus on future success levels.
- Other times, the success criteria are statements of what has been learned.
- Success criteria may include more than one statement per learning intention.

Importantly, the success criteria are not simply tasks to be completed, such as "Complete the science lab" or "Finish the essay." These are tasks that may be used to determine learning, but they are not focused on the success level to be achieved.

Instead, criteria such as those listed in the table below are more likely to produce results.

Success criteria for longer projects often come in the form of rubrics and checklists. These tools can be constructed to focus on multiple areas of success, such as organization, voice, and mechanics in writing. Figure 5 contains a rubric developed for students to self-assess their contributions to group problem-solving tasks. Strong rubrics have indicators and performance descriptors as well as language that students can use to monitor their success. The usefulness of a rubric is limited if students don't have lots of opportunities to use these tools to gauge their own progress.

English Language Arts	<ul><li>I will be able to clearly support my opinion using evidence from the text.</li><li>I can use correct spelling and punctuation so my reader can understand my writing.</li><li>I am able to explain Poe's use of the unreliable narrator in short stories.</li><li>My story has an opening that grabs the reader's attention and an ending with a cliffhanger.</li></ul>
Mathematics	<ul><li>I can put numbers with decimals in order from smallest to largest.</li><li>I can identify all prime numbers between 1 and 100.</li><li>I can make a table of equivalent ratios.</li><li>I can explain why two fractions are equivalent.</li><li>I can explain how to locate the solution to a system of equations by examining a graph.</li></ul>
Science	<ul><li>I can show how buoyancy and density affect an object suspended in a liquid.</li><li>I can name the planets of the solar system in order from their distance from the sun.</li><li>I can explain how changes in velocity affect the movement of an object.</li></ul>
Social Studies	<ul><li>I can compare and contrast how people traveled long ago and today.</li><li>I can identify when, how, and why this country was established.</li><li>I can define necessary conditions for an economy to grow.</li></ul>

FIGURE 5 Self-Assessment Rubric

CRITERIA	REFLECTIVE PRACTITIONER	AWARE PRACTITIONER	REFLECTION NOVICE
Reflective Thinking	The reflection explains the student's own thinking and learning processes, as well as implications for future learning.	The reflection explains the student's thinking about his or her own learning processes.	The reflection does not address the student's thinking and/or learning.
Analysis	The reflection moves beyond simple description of the experience to an analysis of how the experience contributed to student understanding of self, others, and course concepts.	The reflection is an analysis of the learning experience and the value of the derived learning to self or others.	The reflection does not move beyond a description of the learning experience.
Recognizes the Contributions of Others	Recognized and made use of special talents of each team member.	Made some attempt to use special talents of team members.	Does not recognize or use special talents of team members.
Ownership	Accepts responsibility for the team's successes and struggles and states goals for future self-improvement.	Accepts some responsibility for the team's struggles but does not link to future goals.	Accepts minimal responsibility for struggles and blames other team members instead.

Source: Adapted from Buck Institute for Education, http://www.bie.org/objects/cat/rubrics.

Irrespective of the tool used, success criteria provide teachers and students with a goalpost that they can use to monitor progress.

PLC CONVERSATIONS

1. What challenged you in this module?

2. How do you define success and the appropriate level of learning for students?

3. How will we respond if students meet the success criteria in advance of our teaching?

MODELING

The following are examples of success criteria linked to learning intentions in the four grade levels we have been focused on in each of the modeling sections.

GRADE 1: MATH

STANDARD(S)

Solve word problems that call for addition of three whole numbers whose sum is less than or equal to 20 (e.g., by using objects, drawings, and equations with a symbol for the unknown number to represent the problem).

CONCEPTS (NOUNS)

Word problem
Addition
Whole numbers
Sum
Objects
Drawings
Equations
Symbol
Unknown number
Problem

SKILLS (VERBS)

Solve
Use
Represent

LEARNING PROGRESSION

5. Develop an equation to represent the information in the word problem.

LEARNING INTENTIONS

1. I am learning how to write number sentences based on models and pictures.

2. I am learning how to use the number sentences to restate the problem and make sure it matches.

3. I am learning how to look for errors in number sentences.

SUCCESS CRITERIA

1a. I can use words to describe the model and picture I made.
1b. I can write a number sentence with the same meaning as the words.

2a. I can tell the problem in my own words, starting from my number sentence.
2b. I can show where the parts of my number sentence are in my model and my picture.

3a. I can identify mistakes in a number sentence (e.g., number, operation, or sum).
3b. I can write a new number sentence to fix the mistakes I found.

STANDARD(S)

Determine the main idea of a text and explain how it is supported by key details; summarize the text.

CONCEPTS (NOUNS)

Main idea
Key details
Text

SKILLS (VERBS)

Determine
Explain
Summarize

LEARNING PROGRESSION

3. Determine the central or main idea when the author does not provide a topic sentence.

LEARNING INTENTIONS

1. I am learning how to define the concept of *main idea*.

2. I am learning how to locate several ideas and details presented in a text.

3. I am learning how to establish the relative importance of ideas and details presented in the text.

4. I am learning how to identify what the author wants us to remember.

5. I am learning how to determine the main idea, which is the idea that organizes the entire text.

SUCCESS CRITERIA

1. I can list the characteristics of a main idea.

2. I can independently read an informational text and underline key ideas and details.

3. I can rate the ideas and details in terms of their importance from low to high.

4a. I can name the most important details and ideas from the text.
4b. I can decide what the author wants me to remember and justify why I believe so.

5. I can correctly recognize the central idea of the text that indicates the purpose or direction of the text.

GRADE 8: ALGEBRA

STANDARD(S)
Know and apply the properties of integer exponents to generate equivalent numerical expressions.

CONCEPTS (NOUNS)
Properties of integer exponents
Equivalent numerical expressions

SKILLS (VERBS)
Know
Apply
Generate

LEARNING PROGRESSION
1.   Discover and use the product and quotient properties of exponents.

LEARNING INTENTIONS

1.   I am learning how to discover the product property of exponents by expanding and simplifying exponential expressions.

2.   I am learning how to apply the product property of exponents to solve problems.

3.   I am learning how to discover the quotient property of exponents by expanding and simplifying exponential expressions.

4.   I am learning how to apply the quotient property of exponents to solve problems.

SUCCESS CRITERIA

1a. I can expand exponential expressions.
1b. I can simplify multiplication strings by using exponential notation.
1c. I can write a rule for multiplying two powers with the same base.

2a. I can simplify expressions using the product property of exponents.
2b. I can expand expressions using the product property of exponents.

3a. I can cancel like terms in a fraction's numerator and denominator by dividing them to 1.
3b. I can write a rule for dividing two powers with the same base.

4a. I can simplify expressions using the quotient property of exponents.
4b. I can expand expressions using the quotient property of exponents.

STANDARD(S)

Cite strong and thorough textual evidence to support analysis of what the text says explicitly as well as inferences drawn from the text.

CONCEPTS (NOUNS)	SKILLS (VERBS)
Textual evidence	Cite
Analysis of explicit text	Support
Analysis of inferences	Draw from

LEARNING PROGRESSION

4. Use evidence to support an analysis of what the text explicitly says.

LEARNING INTENTIONS	SUCCESS CRITERIA
1. I am learning how to identify important details in the text.	1a. I can list important details in the text. 1b. I can rephrase important details in my own words.
2. I am learning how to identify specific evidence in the text to support the claim.	2a. I can highlight textual evidence on the list that reinforces the claim. 2b. I can provide a rationale for why the evidence supports the claim.
3. I am learning how to explain how the evidence supports the claim.	3. I can summarize in writing how explicit textual evidence supports the claim.

GUIDED PRACTICE

For your first task in the Guided Practice section, consider the possible success criteria generated during a brainstorming session with teachers. Some of these are more appropriate than others. Which of them would be most appropriate? Which would not be as appropriate for the learning intention?

LEARNING INTENTION	SUCCESS CRITERIA	APPROPRIATE OR NOT
I am learning that content on the Internet must be checked for reliability and trustworthiness.	I can use the "about" information to identify authority information.	
	I can identify date information was published.	
	I can rate the accuracy of the information.	
	I can use the domain name to identify credible sources (e.g., .com versus .edu or .gov).	
	I can identify if the information is relevant to the research.	
I am learning that plants are the primary source of matter and energy in most food chains.	I can compare plant and animal cells, noting differences in their structures.	
	I can define *source of matter* and *energy* as they relate to food chains.	
	I can analyze a food chain from a given biome and identify the role that plants play.	
	I can identify producers and consumers in a food chain.	
	I can name common plants that are included in the human food chain.	
I am learning about the role of context in people's response to music.	I can define the various ways people respond to music.	
	I can explore the context of a given piece of music, including social, historical, and cultural influences.	
	I can identify personal preferences in music as informed by your own culture.	
	I can describe the impact of context on audience reception of a given piece of music.	
	I can explain how social and cultural influences shape popular music across time.	

CONTINUED

CONTINUED

Note: For suggested answers, please turn to page 126 or visit the companion website at **resources.corwin.com/teacherclarityplaybook**.

For the second task, craft success criteria for each of the following learning intentions.

LEARNING INTENTION	SUCCESS CRITERIA
I am learning about the impact of water pollution on the environment.	
I am learning about the role of tints and shades in paintings.	
I am learning that shapes can be partitioned into parts with equal areas.	
I am learning that questioning is a way to define unknown words in a text.	

Note: For suggested answers, please turn to page 128 or visit the companion website at **resources.corwin.com/teacherclarityplaybook**.

INDEPENDENT PRACTICE

Now, practice on your own, using your own standard.

STANDARD(S)
The physically literate (individual) demonstrates (competency) in a variety (locomotor skills) and (movement patterns)

CONCEPTS (NOUNS)
- Individual
- Locomotor **skills**
- Movement patterns

SKILLS (VERBS)
- demonstrates

LEARNING PROGRESSION
Explain the importance of locomotor skills and movement patterns

LEARNING INTENTIONS
1. I am learning to define locomotor skills
2. I am learning to define key terms- competency
3. I am learning to list the different locomotor skills
4. I am learning to list the different movement patterns
5. I am learning to put these locomotor skills and movement patterns into action
6.
7.
8.

SUCCESS CRITERIA
- I can list the different locomotor skills
- I can list the different movement patterns
- I can define key terms- competency
- I can put these locomotor skills and movement patterns into action
-
-
-
-

WATCH!

Videos and viewing guide may also be accessed at **resources.corwin.com/ teacherclarityplaybook**

VIDEO 4.2
Module 4 in Action—Elementary
resources.corwin.com/teacherclarityplaybook

VIDEO 4.3
Module 4 in Action—Secondary
resources.corwin.com/teacherclarityplaybook

NOTES

_____

_____

_____

_____

_____

_____

_____

_____

_____

_____

_____

_____

_____

_____

_____

_____

_____

MODULE 5:
MODIFY LEARNING INTENTIONS TO INCLUDE...
Language EXPECTATIONS
LISTENING
SPEAKING
Content
Vocabulary
STRUCTURE
FUNCTION
VIEWING
THE PLAY:
INCLUDE LANGUAGE EXPECTATIONS
WRITING
INTENTIONS
READING

MODULE 5: MODIFYING LEARNING INTENTIONS TO INCLUDE LANGUAGE EXPECTATIONS

◀ VIDEO 5.1 Module 5 Overview
resources.corwin.com/teacherclarityplaybook

Every aspect of learning includes a linguistic demand, be it reading, writing, speaking, listening, or viewing. The daily learning intentions are expressed as statements that signal to students *what* they will be learning. These learning intentions are further enhanced when the language expectations for the lesson are included. Understanding the linguistic demands of the content is critical for mastery of the learning intention and is especially valuable for English learners who are doing double the work, learning content and language simultaneously. Many states have English language development standards that can be used to identify appropriate language learning intentions.

We placed this module here because it's easier to identify the language expectations when you know what success looks like. Oftentimes, the success criteria will indicate the type of language learning needed for students to be successful.

As we will see later in this playbook, the language learning intention also guides the type of data teachers should collect to determine if students have achieved the learning intention. For example, if students are focused on learning about the phases of the moon and the language learning intention focuses on domain-specific vocabulary, then checking for understanding should include vocabulary. Alternatively, if students are expected to describe the phases of the moon, students should be expected to write or discuss each of the phases in order.

To develop the language expectations of the daily learning intention, consider the three possible language requirements:

- Vocabulary
- Language structure
- Language function

These three areas provide guidance in the identification of the linguistic demands of the content. Figure 6 includes several examples of language-related learning intentions for each of these areas.

FIGURE 6 Examples of Language Learning Intention Statements

CONTENT AREA	VOCABULARY	STRUCTURE	FUNCTION
Mathematics	Use *less than*, *equal to*, or *greater than* to compare sets or numbers.	Highlight addition signal words in a word problem.	Describe the relationship between numbers in expanded form and standard form.
Social Studies	Name the routes and explorers on a map.	Sequence the steps of food production using the signal words *first, then, next,* and *finally.*	Justify in a paragraph the ways fire was used for hunting, cooking, and warmth by citing three examples.
Language Arts	Use *who, what,* and *why* to ask a question of your partner.	Identify the verb tenses used in the reading to explain what happened long ago and what will happen in the future.	Explain what organizational pattern was used by the writer and critique its adequacy.

CONTENT AREA	VOCABULARY	STRUCTURE	FUNCTION
Science	Label a diagram of the digestive system (*teeth, mouth, esophagus, stomach, small intestine, large intestine, colon*).	Using the sentence frame "On the one hand, _____. On the other hand, _____," students will demonstrate their knowledge of Earth's layers.	I can inform my team members about three ways that an environment can change.
Art	Use visual analysis terminology (*line, color, balance, form, shape*) to describe a painting.	Use a museum exhibition label form to cite a displayed work of art.	Compare and contrast two paintings from the same time period in a written critique.
Physical Education	Identify body movements used in soccer (*scissor, drag and push, cuts, dribble*).	Use language frames to signal teammates about changing game conditions (e.g., calling for the ball, letting a team member know when there is pressure from an opposing player, signaling encouragement).	Participate in a postgame discussion of successes, challenges, and action steps.

Source: Adapted from Fisher, D., & Frey, N. (2010). "Unpacking the Language Purpose: Vocabulary, Structure, and Function." *TESOL Journal, 1*(3), pp. 315–337.

VOCABULARY LANGUAGE LEARNING EXPECTATIONS

For some lessons, the important linguistic component might be related to the vocabulary of the discipline. This often includes academic words and phrases that students must correctly use in order to accurately represent concepts and ideas. For example, in second grade, the language expectation might be for students to use the terms *time*, *place*, or *location* when describing the setting. Here are other examples of vocabulary language learning expectations:

- Label the map using cardinal directions and cartography terminology.

- Describe the steps for dissection using accurate scientific vocabulary.

- Calculate the abscissa and ordinates to define the point on a two-dimensional graph.

LANGUAGE STRUCTURE LEARNING EXPECTATIONS

For other lessons, students need to focus on grammar, syntax, or signal words. These comprise the structures used in language. A sentence or paragraph frame can organize the structure of the language for students. For example, as part of their conversation with peers, students learning the art of sourcing ideas might use a sentence frame such as this: *While _____ believed _____, others disagreed.*

Additional examples of structure-related language learning intentions include

- Use transitional phrases in your essay to help the reader understand the logic and reasoning of your argument.

- Identify signal words that represent math operations for addition, subtraction, multiplication, and division.

- Construct declarative sentences in French using subject–verb–object word order.

- Use the sentence frames provided to provide your peer with feedback about his or her writing draft.

LANGUAGE FUNCTION LEARNING EXPECTATIONS

A third way to think about the language component is by determining the function of language that is necessary to understand the content. In other words, do students need to justify, persuade, inform, entertain, debate, or hypothesize to understand the lesson? For example, in a discussion about a particular text, the function might be to *justify your answer with evidence from the text*. Examples of language function expectations include

- Summarize the writer's four reasons for supporting the development of a public preschool program for our state.

- Explain to members of your group how the electromagnetic spectrum positively and negatively impacts Earth.

- Based on the data you have analyzed, hypothesize what the introduction of an invasive species of insect would do to the redwoods of the western United States.

- Give instructions to a classmate about how an artist prepares a canvas for painting with oils.

Taken together, these language modifications to the learning intentions assist students in understanding how they will use spoken and written language to learn and to demonstrate mastery of the content.

PLC CONVERSATIONS

1. What challenged you in this module?

2. How can we ensure that students are learning language and content simultaneously in every lesson?

3. How can we create assessments based on the language learning expected?

MODELING

The following are four examples of learning intentions modified to include language expectations. The language expectations are italicized.

STANDARD(S)

Solve word problems that call for addition of three whole numbers whose sum is less than or equal to 20 (e.g., by using objects, drawings, and equations with a symbol for the unknown number to represent the problem).

CONCEPTS (NOUNS)

Word problem
Addition
Whole numbers
Sum
Objects
Drawings
Equations
Symbol
Unknown number
Problem

SKILLS (VERBS)

Solve
Use
Represent

LEARNING PROGRESSION

5. Develop an equation to represent the information in the word problem.

LEARNING INTENTIONS

1. I am learning how to write number sentences based on models and pictures. I am also learning how to *choose from the sentence frames provided to create my sentences.*

2. I am learning how to use the number sentences to restate the problem and make sure it matches. I am also learning how to *use the correct operation words (e.g., plus, add, minus, subtract, equals).*

3. I am learning how to look for errors in number sentences. I am also learning how to *use the word* because *to justify my answer.*

SUCCESS CRITERIA

1a. I can use words to describe the model and picture I made.
1b. I can write a number sentence with the same meaning as the words.

2a. I can tell the problem in my own words starting from my number sentence.
2b. I can show where the parts of my number sentence are in my model and my picture.

3a. I can identify mistakes in a number sentence (e.g., number, operation, or sum).
3b. I can write a new number sentence to fix the mistakes I found.

STANDARD(S)

Determine the main idea of a text and explain how it is supported by key details; summarize the text.

CONCEPTS (NOUNS)

Main idea
Key details
Text

SKILLS (VERBS)

Determine
Explain
Summarize

LEARNING PROGRESSION

3. Determine the central or main idea when the author does not provide a topic sentence.

LEARNING INTENTIONS

1. I am learning how to define the concept of main idea *using target vocabulary*.

2. I am learning how to locate several ideas and details presented in a text *and justify my selections to my peers*.

3. I am learning how to establish the relative importance of ideas and details presented in a text and how to *share my thinking with peers in complete sentences*.

4. I am learning how to identify what the author wants me to remember *and explain the reasons I think so to my peers*.

5. I am learning how to determine the main idea, the idea that organizes the entire text, and how to *explain my ideas in writing using the sentence frames provided*.

SUCCESS CRITERIA

1. I can list the characteristics of a main idea.

2a. I can independently read an informational text and underline key ideas and details.
2b. I can *provide reasons for choices*.

3a. I can rate the ideas and details in terms of their importance from low to high.
3b. I can *explain the importance of the ideas and details that the author selected*.

4a. I can name the most important details and ideas from the text.
4b. I can decide what the author wants me to remember and justify why I believe so.

5. I can correctly recognize the central idea of the text that indicates the purpose or direction of the text.

STANDARD(S)

Know and apply the properties of integer exponents to generate equivalent numerical expressions.

CONCEPTS (NOUNS)

Properties of integer exponents
Equivalent numerical expressions

SKILLS (VERBS)

Know
Apply
Generate

LEARNING PROGRESSION

1. Discover and use the product and quotient properties of exponents.

LEARNING INTENTIONS

1. I am learning how to discover the product property of exponents by expanding and simplifying exponential expressions. I am also learning how to use the terms *base* and *exponent* when discussing with a peer.

2. I am learning how to apply the product property of exponents to solve problems. I am also learning how to precisely state, using technical vocabulary, exponential terms *(e.g., seven to the fifth power—7^5).*

3. I am learning how to discover the quotient property of exponents by expanding and simplifying exponential expressions. I am also learning how to articulate each term and operation in exponential expressions when discussing with peers.

4. I am learning how to apply the quotient property of exponents to solve problems. I am also learning how to carefully describe each property of exponents as it is being used.

SUCCESS CRITERIA

1a. I can expand exponential expressions.
1b. I can simplify multiplication strings by using exponential notation.
1c. I can write a rule for multiplying two powers with the same base.

2a. I can simplify expressions using the product property of exponents.
2b. I can expand expressions using the product property of exponents.

3a. I can cancel like terms in a fraction's numerator and denominator by dividing them to 1.
3b. I can write a rule for dividing two powers with the same base.

4a. I can simplify expressions using the quotient property of exponents.
4b. I can expand expressions using the quotient property of exponents.

GRADE 10: ENGLISH

STANDARD(S)
Cite strong and thorough textual evidence to support analysis of what the text says explicitly as well as inferences drawn from the text.

CONCEPTS (NOUNS)
Textual evidence
Analysis of explicit text
Analysis of inferences

SKILLS (VERBS)
Cite
Support
Draw from

LEARNING PROGRESSION
4. Use evidence to support an analysis of what the text explicitly says.

LEARNING INTENTIONS

1. I am learning how to identify important details in the text and how to *share my thinking with a partner using complete sentences.*

2. I am learning how to identify specific evidence in the text to support my claim and *justify my thinking with a triad.*

3. I am learning how to explain how the evidence supports my claim *using the frame "I believe ____ because the text says ____." I am also learning how to use transitional phrases (e.g., for example, for instance, specifically).*

SUCCESS CRITERIA

1a. I can list important details in the text.
1b. Rephrase important details in my own words.

2a. I can highlight textual evidence on the list that reinforces the claim.
2b. Provide a rationale for why your evidence supports your claim.

3. I can summarize in writing how explicit textual evidence supports your claim.

GUIDED PRACTICE

For your first task, consider the following language learning expectations presented and identify if they are more aligned with student needs in vocabulary, language structure, or language function.

EXAMPLES	V	S	F
Kindergarten: Language Arts **Content learning intention:** I am learning how to retell a story. **Language learning intention:** I am learning how to retell the story and include at least three events.			✓
Grade 1: Math **Content learning intention:** I am learning about how many tens and ones are in a set. **Language learning intention:** I am learning how to apply the sentence frame "____ sets of ten and ____ones equal ____." (Ex: "Three sets of tens and 2 ones equal 32.")		✓	
Grade 2: Life Science **Content learning intention:** I am learning about life cycles. **Language learning intention:** I am learning how to summarize the similarities and differences between the life cycle of a frog and a butterfly.			✓
Grade 3: Language Arts **Content learning intention:** I am learning about genres and text types. **Language learning intention:** I am learning how to justify why a passage is poetry, fiction, or nonfiction.	✓		
Grade 4: Earth Science **Content learning intention:** I am learning about landslides, volcanic eruptions, and earthquakes and how they change rocks. **Language learning intention:** I am learning how to use technical vocabulary to discuss how rocks reflect the processes that formed them.	✓		
Grade 5: Social Studies **Content learning intention:** I am learning about the major causes of the American Revolution. **Language learning intention:** I am learning how to apply compare/contrast signal words in a written explanation of the major causes of the American Revolution.		✓	
Grade 6: Math **Content learning intention:** I am learning about relevant and irrelevant information in word problems. **Language learning intention:** I am learning how to explain which aspects of a word problem are relevant and irrelevant.		✓	✓

V = Vocabulary (specialized, technical)

S = Language Structure (grammar, syntax, signal words, frames)

F = Language Function (instrumental, regulatory, interactional, personal, imaginative, heuristic, representational)

Note: For suggested answers, please turn to page 128 or visit the companion website at **resources.corwin.com/teacherclarityplaybook**.

CONTINUED →

CONTINUED

For the second task, modify each of the following learning intentions to include the language expectation identified.

LEARNING INTENTION	LANGUAGE EXPECTATION	MODIFIED VERSION OR LANGUAGE EXPECTATION
I am learning how to partition shapes into parts with equal areas.	Vocabulary	
I am learning how to identify reliable and trustworthy content from the Internet.	Function	
I am learning how to ask questions about unknown words in a text.	Structure	
I am learning how to identify the impact of water pollution on the environment	Function	
I am learning how to demonstrate and explain how responses to music are informed by the context (such as social and cultural).	Vocabulary	
I am learning how to describe the ways that artists use tints and shades in painting.	Structure	
I am learning how to predict the geological features that result from specific plate boundaries (subduction zones, divergent margins, and transform margins).	Function	

Note: For suggested answers, please turn to page 129 or visit the companion website at **resources.corwin.com/teacherclarityplaybook**.

INDEObPENDENT PRACTICE

For your independent practice, complete the following template with one of your standards, the concepts, skills, learning progressions, and learning intentions.

STANDARD(S)

CONCEPTS (NOUNS)   SKILLS (VERBS)

LEARNING PROGRESSION

MODIFIED LEARNING INTENTIONS

1.

2.

3.

4.

5.

6.

7.

8.

WATCH!

Videos and viewing guide may also be accessed at **resources.corwin.com/teacherclarityplaybook**

VIDEO 5.2
Module 5 in Action—Elementary
resources.corwin.com/teacherclarityplaybook

VIDEO 5.3
Module 5 in Action—Secondary
resources.corwin.com/teacherclarityplaybook

NOTES

_____

_____

_____

_____

_____

_____

_____

_____

_____

_____

_____

_____

_____

_____

_____

_____

_____

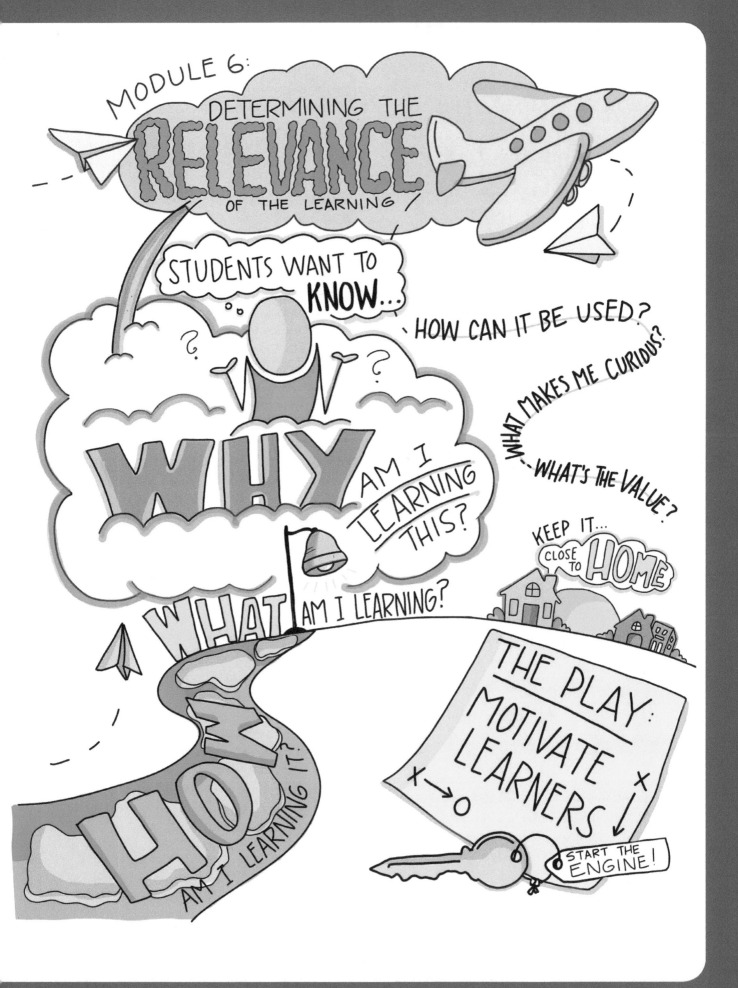

MODULE 6: DETERMINING THE RELEVANCE OF THE LEARNING

◄ **VIDEO 6.1 Module 6 Overview**
resources.corwin.com/teacherclarityplaybook

We can't leave the subject of learning intentions and success criteria before addressing the issue of relevancy in learning. Learning intentions and success criteria address the acquisition and consolidation of skills and concepts, but relevancy addresses motivation to learn. All learners need to have some insight into *why* they are learning something. We believe that students should be able to answer, and ask, these questions of each lesson:

1. What am I learning today?
2. Why am I learning this?
3. How will I know that I learned it?

The stated daily learning intentions address the first question, and success criteria supply the tools needed to answer the third question as students gauge their own progress. But the second question is about relevancy. This section examines ways to make learning relevant to learners.

RELEVANCY IS AN ENGINE FOR LEARNING

Some learning purposes come with relevancy baked into them, such as successfully completing a driver's education course in order to gain a permit or license. But the relevancy of much of the school-based knowledge we teach is not so readily apparent to the learner. It can be a struggle to frame the relevancy of content if one possesses a belief that everything needs to

lead to a distant and aspirational ending, such as focusing on graduating from college when you're still in fourth grade. Quite frankly, a lot of what we teach doesn't really fit into the driver's license kind of scenario, and when it's too far in the distance, it's not very motivating anyway. Relevancy needs to be closer to home. Why are syllables important? *Because they help us read big words.* Why do we need to know the difference between a simile and a metaphor? *So we can use these techniques in our own writing to express ideas without being too obvious.* Why are we learning to balance equations in chemistry? *Because no substance on Earth can exist if it violates the law of conservation of matter.* Taking the time to address relevancy fosters motivation and deepens learning as students begin to make connections to larger concepts. In other words, an understanding of the relevancy of their learning moves students forward from declarative (factual) knowledge through procedural and conditional knowledge—from *what to how to when.*

HOW TO COMMUNICATE RELEVANCE

In general, we think that there are three ways to make learning relevant. The first is how the information can be used outside the walls of the classroom. As we noted earlier, it can't be too far in the distance, but understanding that learning has utility beyond the classroom can hone students' attention. When a student understands that writing introductions can be useful in letters of application for jobs, she or he is more interested in what English teachers have to say. When a math student understands that quadratic equations help the taco shop owner make decisions about production and cost, the purpose for learning the content becomes clearer.

A second way to make learning relevant is to involve students directly. Ask questions of students about what they want to learn. Student learning is driven by the questions formulated with and by the learner. Therefore, an important role of the teacher is to foster questions and dialogue to meaningful experiences that allow them to interact with you and one another. When presenting the daily learning intentions and success criteria, add a sentence frame such as, "This will help me to _____," and then dialogue with students in order to co-construct relevancy. At the end of a lesson, ask students, "Based on today's learning, what are you curious about? Has this content raised any questions for you?"

A third way that teachers can make learning relevant is to note the value of the lesson in becoming an educated member of the community. For some students, this is a bit of a stretch, but others enjoy knowing things that other people know and what other people don't know. Use newsworthy examples to show how chemistry concepts figure into climate change, or how the controversial nature of some monuments causes contemporary reexamination of historical events. Discuss how Shakespeare influenced the English language and invented new words and sayings that are used today. What adolescent could resist knowing that the Bard himself invented the word *puking*?

Sometimes, relevance is born of utility— "Learning this means we can do things we couldn't do before." Completing the square and subsequent quadratic formula that it proves, for instance, makes a previously unfactorable, and hence unsolvable, quadratic equation suddenly solvable. In this same vein, a task that exposes an inability can spur the need (and therefore relevance) of new learning. In this sense, relevance isn't communicated by the teacher insomuch as it is manufactured within the student (by the design of the teacher). This is about creating or exposing the cognitive dissonance and disequilibrium so that we can stimulate a student's natural response—learning.

Unfortunately, conversations about relevance are often skipped, and students have no idea why they are learning the content. Compliant learners might persist anyway, but less motivated students will probably forget everything because they did not understand the value of the experience. In other words, students want to know the following:

- Why am I learning this?
- How does this connect with my previous learning and what I already know?
- How will this help me reach the learning intention and success criteria?

PLC CONVERSATIONS

1. What challenged you in this module?

2. What makes learning relevant for our students? What do we know about them that we could use to make connections?

3. How can we develop internal motivation in our students?

MODELING

See the following four examples with talking points on relevance included. We have modified each of the previously created lessons to include ideas that might make the lesson relevant for students.

GRADE 1: MATH

STANDARD(S)

Solve word problems that call for addition of three whole numbers whose sum is less than or equal to 20 (e.g., by using objects, drawings, and equations with a symbol for the unknown number to represent the problem).

CONCEPTS (NOUNS)

Word problem
Addition
Whole numbers
Sum
Objects
Drawings
Equations
Symbol
Unknown number
Problem

SKILLS (VERBS)

Solve
Use
Represent

LEARNING PROGRESSION

5. Develop an equation to represent the information in the word problem.

LEARNING INTENTIONS

1. I am learning how to write number sentences based on models and pictures. I am also learning how to choose from the sentence frames provided to create my sentences.

SUCCESS CRITERIA

1a. I can use words to describe the model and picture I made.

1b. I can write a number sentence with the same meaning as the words.

TALKING POINTS ON RELEVANCE

1a. We want to be able to set these problems up as numbers and equations so math can help us solve them.

1b. We want to figure out how to solve these interesting problems and understand why our answer makes sense.

2. I am learning how to use the number sentences to restate the problem and make sure it matches. I am also learning how to use the correct operation words (e.g., plus, add, minus, subtract, equals).	2a. I can tell the problem in my own words starting from my number sentence. 2b. I can show where the parts of my number sentence are in my model and my picture.	2a. Mathematicians use numbers and symbols, not just words. 2b. It's easier to add when we see the number and not just the words. 2c. It helps us check our answers to see if we are right.
3. I am learning how to look for errors in number sentences. I am also learning how to use the word *because* to justify my answer.	3a. I can identify mistakes in a number sentence (e.g., number, operation, or sum). 3b. I can write a new number sentence to fix the mistakes I found.	3. It is important to be able to tell when something is not correct. When we learn how to find mistakes in math work, we get better at fixing our own mistakes and helping others fix theirs. Nobody wants to believe something that is not true.

GRADE 4: ELA

STANDARD(S)
Determine the main idea of a text and explain how it is supported by key details; summarize the text.

CONCEPTS (NOUNS)
Main idea
Key details
Text

SKILLS (VERBS)
Determine
Explain
Summarize

LEARNING PROGRESSION
3. Determine the central or main idea when the author does not provide a topic sentence.

CONTINUED

LEARNING INTENTIONS	SUCCESS CRITERIA	TALKING POINTS ON RELEVANCE
1. I am learning how to define the concept of *main idea* using target vocabulary.	1. I can list the characteristics of a main idea.	1a. You can't remember everything in the text, so the main idea helps you remember important things. 1b. When you know what the main idea is, you can make sure you have a main idea in your own writing.
2. I am learning how to locate several ideas and details presented in a text and justify my selections to my peers.	2. I can independently read an informational text and underline key ideas and details. 2b. I can provide reasons for choices.	2a. Identifying ideas and details helps you organize your thinking so that you can use the information from the text later. 2b. When you provide reasons for your choices, people can decide if they agree or disagree with your ideas.
3. I am learning how to establish the relative importance of ideas and details presented in a text and how to share my thinking with my peers in complete sentences.	3a. I can rate the ideas and details in terms of their importance from low to high. 3b. I can explain the importance of the ideas and details that the author selected.	3a. Knowing the difference between interesting ideas and important details helps you find the main idea. 3b. Collecting interesting ideas and important details is useful when you write about a reading.

4. I am learning how to identify what the author wants me to remember and explain the reasons I think so to my peers.	4a. I can name the most important details and ideas from the text. 4b. I can decide what the author wants me to remember and justify why I believe so.	4a. Knowing what the author wants you to remember allows you to understand the author's perspective to decide if you agree or disagree.
5. I am learning how to determine the main idea, which is the idea that organizes the entire text, and how to explain my ideas in writing using the sentence frames provided.	5. I can correctly recognize the central idea of the text that indicates the purpose or direction of the text.	5a. Knowing the main idea helps you remember information from a text. 5b. When you have discovered the main idea, you can write about the text using evidence from the text, which is something that people have to do all of the time when they are at work.

GRADE 8: ALGEBRA

STANDARD(S)

Know and apply the properties of integer exponents to generate equivalent numerical expressions.

CONCEPTS (NOUNS)

Properties of integer exponents
Equivalent numerical expressions

SKILLS (VERBS)

Know
Apply
Generate

LEARNING PROGRESSION

1. Discover and use the product and quotient properties of exponents.

CONTINUED

LEARNING INTENTIONS	SUCCESS CRITERIA	TALKING POINTS ON RELEVANCE
1. I am learning how to discover the product property of exponents by expanding and simplifying exponential expressions. I am also learning how to use the terms *base* and *exponent* when discussing with a peer.	1a. I can expand exponential expressions. 1b. I can simplify multiplication strings by using exponential notation. 1c. I can write a rule for multiplying two powers with the same base.	1a. Exponential notation allows us to denote complicated quantities in a simpler way. 1b. The product property is a tool that mathematicians use to make very large calculations much simpler.
2. I am learning how to apply the product property of exponents to solve problems. I am also learning how to precisely state exponential terms (e.g., seven to the fifth power—7^5), using technical vocabulary.	2a. I can simplify expressions using the product property of exponents. 2b. I can expand expressions using the product property of exponents.	2a. As we become better mathematicians and discover more tools, we become more efficient and can do more work with less effort. 2b. Scientists use the product property when multiplying very large or very small measurements in scientific notation.
3. I am learning how to discover the quotient property of exponents by expanding and simplifying exponential expressions. I am also learning how to articulate each term and operation in exponential expressions when discussing with peers.	3a. I can cancel like terms in a fraction's numerator and denominator by dividing them to 1. 3b. I can write a rule for dividing two powers with the same base.	3a. Math is all about looking for patterns and taking advantage of their structure. 3b. As you move on to more advanced mathematics, "shortcuts" like the quotient property aren't just convenient—they're necessary!

4. I am learning how to apply the quotient property of exponents to solve problems. I am also learning how to carefully describe each property of exponents as it is being used.	4a. I can simplify expressions using the quotient property of exponents. 4b. I can expand expressions using the quotient property of exponents.	4a. How many times farther away from Earth is the nearest galaxy than the center of our own galaxy? The quotient property can help!

GRADE 10: ENGLISH

STANDARD(S)

Cite strong and thorough textual evidence to support analysis of what the text says explicitly as well as inferences drawn from the text.

CONCEPTS (NOUNS)

Textual evidence

Analysis of explicit text

Analysis of inferences

SKILLS (VERBS)

Cite

Support

Draw from

LEARNING PROGRESSION

4. Use evidence to support an analysis of what the text explicitly says.

LEARNING INTENTIONS

1. I am learning how to identify important details in the text and share my thinking with a partner using complete sentences.

SUCCESS CRITERIA

1a. I can list important details in the text.

1b. I can rephrase important details in my own words

TALKING POINTS ON RELEVANCE

1a. Understanding the important details helps you make sense of what you read.

1b. Writers need to present ideas logically so their readers understand.

CONTINUED

2. I am learning how to identify specific evidence in the text to support my claim and justify my thinking with a triad.

2a. I can highlight textual evidence on the list that reinforces the claim.

2b. I can provide a rationale for why my evidence supports my claim.

2a. Identifying evidence helps you back up or justify your claim.

2b. When you use accurate evidence to support your claim, you become a stronger writer and speaker on a text.

3. I am learning how to explain how the evidence supports my claim using the frame "I believe ____ because the text says ____." I am also learning how to use transitional phrases (e.g., for example, for instance, specifically).

3. I can summarize in writing how explicit textual evidence supports my claim.

3. These short draft summaries will be useful when you write your literary analysis essay.

GUIDED PRACTICE

For your first task, read each learning intentions and the potential talking points on relevance. Identify which of the talking points would be most effective for students to engage with the content

LEARNING INTENTION	RELEVANCE	WHICH IS BETTER? WHY?
I am learning how to partition shapes into parts with equal areas.	1. You will need this on the upcoming test. 2. When we make fractional parts, we want to be fair and have each part the same size.	
I am learning how to identify reliable and trustworthy content from the Internet.	1. Doing so makes sure that you are not a victim of crimes or lies. 2. If you know what is trustworthy, you become a critical consumer of information.	
I am learning how to ask questions about unknown words in a text.	1. Readers work to make meaning of the texts they read. 2. Asking questions helps you pay attention to what the author is saying. 3. When you find unknown words, you can add them to your vocabulary journal.	
I am learning how to identify the impact of water pollution on the environment.	1. When you understand the causes and impact, you can help contribute to a healthy environment. 2. This unit will prepare you for the next one when we study the water cycle.	

CONTINUED

I am learning how to describe how artists use tints and shades in painting.	1. These are important words that you should know and be able to use on your own. 2. These concepts help you understand artistic style so that you can discuss art with others.	
I am learning how to predict the resulting geological features that occur with specific plate boundaries (subduction zones, divergent margins, and transform margins).	1. This will help when you go to buy a house so that you are not buying near a dangerous area. 2. This is another opportunity for us to develop our predictive skills. 3. You will do better on the state test if you know this content.	

Note: For suggested answers, please turn to page 130 or visit the companion website at **resources.corwin.com/teacherclarityplaybook**.

For your second task, review the learning intentions from the last unit and identify potential talking points for making these expectations relevant for students.

EXAMPLES	POTENTIAL TALKING POINTS ON RELEVANCE
Kindergarten: Language Arts **Content learning intention:** I am learning to identify the important events after hearing a story. **Language learning intention:** I am learning to retell the story and include at least three events.	
Grade 1: Math **Content learning intention:** I am learning about how many tens and ones are in a set. **Language learning intention:** I am learning to apply the sentence frame "____ sets of ten and ____ ones equal ____." (Ex: "Three sets of ten and 2 ones equal 32.")	

Grade 2: Life Science **Content learning intention:** I am learning to compare and contrast the life cycles. **Language learning intention:** I am learning to summarize the similarities and differences between the life cycle of a frog and a butterfly.	
Grade 3: Language Arts **Content learning intention:** I am learning to evaluate key features of common texts. **Language learning intention:** I am learning to justify why a passage is poetry, fiction, or nonfiction.	
Grade 4: Earth Science **Content learning intention:** I am learning to recognize how landslides, volcanic eruptions, and earthquakes cause changes to rocks. **Language learning intention:** I am learning to use technical vocabulary to discuss how rocks reflect the processes that formed them.	
Grade 5: Social Studies **Content learning intention:** I am learning to analyze the major causes of the American Revolution. **Language learning intention:** I am learning to apply compare/contrast signal words in a written explanation of the major causes of the American Revolution.	
Grade 6: Math **Content:** I am learning to differentiate between relevant and irrelevant information in word problems. **Language learning intention:** I am learning to explain which aspects of a word problem are relevant and irrelevant.	

Note: For suggested answers, please turn to page 131 or visit the companion website at **resources.corwin.com/teacherclarityplaybook**.

INDEPENDENT PRACTICE

STANDARD(S)

CONCEPTS (NOUNS)

SKILLS (VERBS)

LEARNING PROGRESSION

LEARNING INTENTIONS

SUCCESS CRITERIA

TALKING POINTS ON RELEVANCE

WATCH!

Videos and viewing guide may also be accessed at **resources.corwin.com/ teacherclarityplaybook**

VIDEO 6.2
Module 6 in Action—Elementary
resources.corwin.com/teacherclarityplaybook

VIDEO 6.3
Module 6 in Action—Secondary
resources.corwin.com/teacherclarityplaybook

NOTES

NOTES

_____

_____

_____

_____

_____

_____

_____

_____

_____

_____

_____

_____

_____

_____

_____

_____

_____

_____

_____

_____

_____

_____

_____

_____

_____

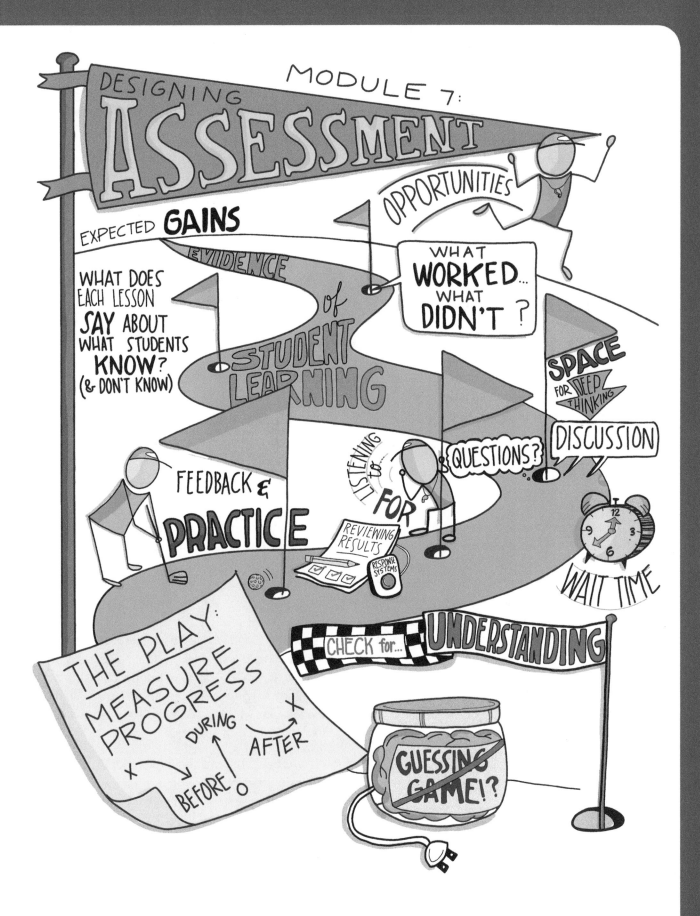

MODULE 7: DESIGNING ASSESSMENT OPPORTUNITIES

◄ VIDEO 7.1 Module 7 Overview
resources.corwin.com/teacherclarityplaybook

As educators, we apportion information so that students can act upon their growing knowledge of the discipline, and we measure their progress throughout to see whether they are making expected gains. As part of effective practice, teachers routinely check for understanding throughout the learning process. This is most commonly accomplished by asking questions, analyzing written tasks, and administering low-stakes quizzes to measure the extent to which students are acquiring new information and skills. But it's one thing to gather information (we're good at that); it's another thing to respond in meaningful ways and then plan for subsequent instruction. Without processes to provide students with solid feedback that yields deeper understanding, checking for understanding devolves into a game of "Guess What's in the Teacher's Brain." And without ways to look for patterns across students, formative assessments become a frustrating academic exercise.

CHECK FOR UNDERSTANDING USING FORMATIVE EVALUATION

Assessment is assessment. Any assessment can be used formatively or summatively. In other words, there's nothing magical in the tool itself; it's what you do with it (or don't do with it) that matters. Using assessments for the purpose of formative evaluation casts a light on teaching practices. It has the potential to be eye-opening—to help teachers consider what worked and what didn't as they carefully examine the evidence of student progress.

CHECK FOR UNDERSTANDING IN EVERY LESSON

No lesson should occur without gathering and analyzing some form of data to signal what it is that students currently know and do not know. These are not isolated measures of a given student's achievement at a single point in time but rather reveal the overall trajectory of his or her learning experience.

CHECK FOR UNDERSTANDING THROUGH DIALOGIC INSTRUCTION

Student discussion is critical for learning. Teachers who create space for students to pose questions, wrestle with complex issues, clarify thinking, speculate, probe, disagree, resolve problems, and reach consensus are employing a dialogic approach to instruction. Unlike the initiate–respond–evaluate cycle of teacher questioning followed by student recitation of the answer (Cazden, 1988), this form of instruction assumes a higher level of authority on the part of the learners, who co-construct knowledge under the guidance of a teacher.

A teacher's nonverbal signals and compassionate listening can encourage students to take risks, publicly speculate, ask questions, and pose arguments. Teacher listening during student discussions is challenging because we're simultaneously doing two things—we are listening *to* and listening *for*. Listening *to* students is the act of locating identity within their utterances. In doing so, we consider how their insights and questions in turn inform us about who they are as individuals. At the same time, we are listening *for* the turns in the conversation that signal content understandings and misconceptions.

We encourage teachers to adopt discussion techniques for getting students to extend their responses. Teachers are able to glean much more about what students know and don't know when they respond to a question. These discussion techniques should become a habit you develop to foster discussion:

- *Revoice student comments:* "So if I understand you correctly, you're saying ..."
- *Emphasize key points:* "I hope everyone had a chance to hear that. Could you repeat that?"
- *Give them time to think:* "Take your time. Say more about this idea."
- *Turn questions back to the class.* "You've raised an interesting point. I'd like to hear from others about how you would respond to Evan's question."
- *Ask for evidence:* "Could you show us in the text where you found that?" Or "Could you show your partner on the graph where you used that in your solution?"

These discussion techniques should be punctuated by wait time, both after posing a thought-provoking question (Wait Time 1) and again after a student responds (Wait Time 2). The first wait time allows students to process and contemplate the question, while the second wait time provides the speaker with the space to elaborate on his or her answer. Although less readily recognized, the practice of ensuring wait time allows the teacher to also process the conversation and results in increased quality of teacher questions. Equipped with the tools to listen carefully to children, to facilitate and guide discussion, and to provide them the space and time to think, teachers can leverage dialogic instruction to deepen knowledge.

CHECK FOR UNDERSTANDING THROUGH WRITING

Short writing prompts during the lesson can allow teachers to gauge student thinking as they check for understanding.

- *Admit Slips*: Upon entering the classroom, students respond to an assigned topic such as "Who was Napoleon, and why should we care?" or "Describe the digestive process," or "Why are irrational numbers important in science and engineering?"
- *Crystal Ball*: Students describe what they think class will be about, what might happen next in the novel they're reading, or what might be the next step in a science lab. For example, while reading a novel, the English teacher pauses and invites students to predict what the character will do next.
- *Yesterday's News*: Students summarize the information presented the day before, either from a film, lecture, discussion, or reading.

One of the most common ways to check for understanding though writing is in the form of exit slips. These writing prompts should stem from the day's stated learning intention and success criteria. For instance, if the learning intention was to "Name four reasons the Pilgrims left England for the New World," then the exit slip should be directly linked. Raise the value of exit slips by asking students to self-assess their understanding. After reviewing the success criteria, students submit exit tickets in one of four categories:

1. I'm just learning (I need more help).
2. I'm almost there (I need more practice).

3. I own it (I can work independently).

4. I'm a pro (I can teach others)!

Students' self-assessment of their level of understanding can provide valuable information for teachers. And this information can be used for reteaching some students (such as those in category 1) or mobilizing peer tutors (such as those in category 4). We will explore this in more detail in the Establishing Mastery of Standards module.

CHECK FOR UNDERSTANDING WITH FORMATIVE PRACTICE TESTING

An underused method is formative practice testing, in which students take short quizzes to understand their command of the subject or topic. These formative practice tests are low-stakes and not part of the student's grade, as the emphasis here is on practice to gain self-knowledge of learning gaps. Formative practice evaluation is not confined to administration of paper-and-pencil or online quizzes. Classroom audience response systems are another form and have the added benefit of providing instant results. The true value is through the insights students gain about their current level of understanding. Therefore, reviewing results with students is critical. When students understand the results of the practice tests, they can focus their studying to improve their future performance.

There are many, many more ways to check for understanding. The point here is that teachers should check for understanding during each lesson. It's an important part of teacher clarity. In essence, we're checking to see if the learning experience stuck. Teachers should collect evidence of students' progress toward the learning intention and success criteria so that they can make instructional decisions for the following lesson. In this way, student learning becomes central to the teaching process itself, and the assessment tools truly are formative evaluations of student performance and the impact that the teaching has had.

PLC CONVERSATIONS

1. What challenged you in this module?

2. What assessments and checks for understanding are we already using that we can continue to use? What new tools do we need to explore?

3. How can we ensure that our assessments provide feedback to us about the impact of our teaching?

MODELING

The following are four examples of a standard broken down into learning intentions, success criteria, and talking points on relevance, with assessment opportunities listed as well.

GRADE 1: MATH

STANDARD(S)

Solve word problems that call for addition of three whole numbers whose sum is less than or equal to 20 (e.g., by using objects, drawings, and equations with a symbol for the unknown number to represent the problem).

CONCEPTS (NOUNS)

Word problem
Addition
Whole numbers
Sum
Objects
Drawings
Equations
Symbol
Unknown number
Problem

SKILLS (VERBS)

Solve
Use
Represent

LEARNING PROGRESSION

5. Develop an equation to represent the information in the word problem.

LEARNING INTENTIONS	SUCCESS CRITERIA	TALKING POINTS ON RELEVANCE	ASSESSMENT OPPORTUNITIES
1. I am learning how to write number sentences based on models and pictures. I am also learning how to choose from the sentence frames provided to create my sentences.	1a. I can use words to describe the model and picture I made. 1b. I can write a number sentence with the same meaning as the words.	1a. We want to set these problems up as numbers and equations so that we can use math to solve them. 1b. We want to figure out how to solve these interesting problems and understand why our answer makes sense.	1a. Inclusive response opportunity: Students hold up dry erase boards with number sentences written on them. 1b. Use number and operation cards to build their sentences.

CONTINUED

2. I am learning how to use the number sentences to restate the problem and make sure it matches. I am also learning how to use the correct operation words (e.g., plus, add, minus, subtract, equals).	2a. I can tell the problem in my own words starting from my number sentence. 2b. I can show where the parts of my number sentence are in my model and my picture.	2a. Mathematicians use numbers and symbols, not just words. 2b. It's easier to add when we see the number and not just the words. 2c. It helps us check our answers to see if we are right.	2. Listen in on partner conversations as students restate problems and justify their answers.
3. I am learning how to look for errors in number sentences. I am also learning how to use the word *because* to justify my answer.	3a. I can identify mistakes in a number sentence (e.g., number, operation, or sum). 3b. I can write a new number sentence to fix the mistakes I found.	3. There might not be someone to help us find our mistakes, so we need to learn how to discover when we make a mistake and fix it.	3a. Listen in on partner conversations to identify correct and incorrect responses. 3b. Students glue strips of paper into their math journal that have incorrect number sentences typed out. Students identify errors in number sentences in their journal.

STANDARD(S)

Determine the main idea of a text and explain how it is supported by key details; summarize the text.

CONCEPTS (NOUNS)

Main idea
Key details
Text

SKILLS (VERBS)

Determine
Explain
Summarize

LEARNING PROGRESSION

3. Determine the central or main idea when the author does not provide a topic sentence.

LEARNING INTENTIONS	SUCCESS CRITERIA	TALKING POINTS ON RELEVANCE	ASSESSMENT OPPORTUNITIES
1. I am learning how to define the concept of *main idea* using target vocabulary.	1. I can list the characteristics of a main idea.	1a. You can't remember everything in the text, so the main idea helps you remember important things. 1b. When you know what the main idea is, you can make sure you have a main idea in your own writing.	1a. Listen in on partner conversations as students discuss the concept. 1b. In their writing journal, students will include their list of characteristics of the main idea, including examples from the shared text that the whole class read.
2. I am learning how to locate several ideas and details presented in a text and justify my selections to my peers.	2. I can independently read an informational text and underline key ideas and details. 2b. I can provide reasons for choices.	2a. Identifying ideas and details helps you organize your thinking so that you can use the information from the text later. 2b. When you provide reasons for your choices, people can decide if they agree or disagree with your ideas.	2a. The text is glued into students' writing journals, and they underline key ideas and details. 2b. Listen in on partner conversations as students discuss their selections of ideas and details.

CONTINUED

3. I am learning how to establish the relative importance of ideas and details presented in a text and share my thinking with peers in complete sentences.	3a. I can rate the ideas and details in terms of their importance from low to high. 3b. I can explain the importance of the ideas and details selected.	3a. Knowing the difference between interesting ideas and important details helps you find the main idea. 3b. Collecting interesting ideas and important details are useful when you write about a reading.	3a. In their writing journals, students rank the ideas and details from lowest to highest and include a written rationale for the order they have identified. 3b. Listen in on partner conversations as students discuss their ratings.
4. I am learning how to identify what the author wants me to remember and explain the reasons I think so to my peers.	4a. I can name the most important details and ideas from the text. 4b. I can decide what the author wants me to remember and justify why I believe so.	4a. Knowing what the author wants you to remember allows you to understand the author's perspective to decide if you agree or disagree.	4. Listen in on partner conversations as students discuss their most important details and the reasons that they selected those details.
5. I am learning how to determine the main idea, which is the idea that organizes the entire text, and explain my ideas in writing using the sentence frames provided.	5. I can correctly recognize the central idea of the text that indicates the purpose or direction of the text.	5a. Knowing the main idea helps you remember information from a text. 5b. When you have discovered the main idea, you can write about the text using evidence from it, which is something that people have to do all of the time when they are at work.	5. Given a new text selection, students identify the main idea and write in their journals about the reasons they believe that this is the most important thing that the author wants them to remember.

GRADE 8: ALGEBRA

STANDARD(S)
Know and apply the properties of integer exponents to generate equivalent numerical expressions.

CONCEPTS (NOUNS)
Properties of integer exponents
Equivalent numerical expressions

SKILLS (VERBS)
Know
Apply
Generate

LEARNING PROGRESSION:
1. Discover and use the product and quotient properties of exponents.

LEARNING INTENTIONS	SUCCESS CRITERIA	TALKING POINTS ON RELEVANCE	ASSESSMENT OPPORTUNITIES
1. I am learning how to discover the product property of exponents by expanding and simplifying exponential expressions. I am also learning how to use the terms *base* and *exponent* when discussing with a peer.	1a. I can expand exponential expressions. 1b. I can simplify multiplication strings by using exponential notation. 1c. I can write a rule for multiplying two powers with the same base.	1a. Exponential notation allows us to denote complicated quantities in a simpler way. 1b. The product property is a tool that mathematicians use to make very large calculations much simpler.	1a. Listen as groups work through the task. Are students accurately identifying the base and exponent of exponential terms? 1b. Students will record their work for the task in their math notebooks. Are they properly expanding and simplifying exponential expressions? 1c. Culminate the day with a whole-class discussion describing the patterns students noticed. Can they write the product property as a rule from their experience?

CONTINUED

2. I am learning how to apply the product property of exponents to solve problems. I am also learning how to precisely state exponential terms (e.g., seven to the fifth power—7^5) using technical vocabulary.

2a. I can simplify expressions using the product property of exponents.

2b. I can expand expressions using the product property of exponents.

2a. As we become better mathematicians and discover more tools, we become more efficient and can do more work with less effort.

2b. Scientists use the product property when multiplying very large or very small measurements in scientific notation.

2a. Listen as partners discuss problems. Are they precisely stating exponential terms?

2b. Use peer-assisted-reflection (PAR), in which students work through a problem, trade work, and provide feedback through written annotations.

3. I am learning how to discover the quotient property of exponents by expanding and simplifying exponential expressions. I am also learning how to articulate each term and operation in exponential expressions when discussing with peers.

3a. I can cancel like terms in a fraction's numerator and denominator by dividing them to 1.

3b. I can write a rule for dividing two powers with the same base.

3a. Math is all about looking for patterns and taking advantage of their structure.

3b. As you move on to more advanced mathematics, "shortcuts" like the quotient property aren't just convenient, they're necessary!

3a. Listen as groups work through the task. Are they articulating each term and operation in exponential expressions?

3b. Scan each group's work for alignment to success criteria.

3c. Students will summarize their discovery from the task by writing a rule for dividing two powers with the same base in their math notebooks.

| 4. I am learning how to apply the quotient property of exponents to solve problems. I am also learning how to carefully describe each property of exponents as it is being used. | 4a. I can simplify expressions using the quotient property of exponents.

4b. I can expand expressions using the quotient property of exponents. | 4a. How many times farther away from Earth is the nearest galaxy than the center of our own galaxy? The quotient property can help! | 4a. Students paste a pre-solved problem in their math notebooks and annotate each step using complete sentences. Are they carefully describing each property of exponents as it is being used.

4b. At certain checkpoints throughout the lesson, students display solutions on individual whiteboards.

4c. Students submit exit tickets with problems aligned to success criteria and self-assess based on confidence. |

GRADE 10: ENGLISH

STANDARD(S)

Cite strong and thorough textual evidence to support analysis of what the text says explicitly as well as inferences drawn from the text.

CONCEPTS (NOUNS)	SKILLS (VERBS)
Textual evidence	Cite
Analysis of explicit text	Support
Analysis of inferences	Draw from

LEARNING PROGRESSION

4. Use evidence to support an analysis of what the text explicitly says.

CONTINUED

LEARNING INTENTIONS	SUCCESS CRITERIA	TALKING POINTS ON RELEVANCE	ASSESSMENT OPPORTUNITIES
1. I am learning how to identify important details in the text and share my thinking with a partner using complete sentences.	1a. I can list important details in the text. 1b. I can rephrase important details in my own words.	1a. Understanding the important details helps you make sense of what you read. 1b. Writers need to present ideas logically so their readers understand.	1a. Students write the important details in their writing journals. 1b. Students use sentence strips or sticky notes to sort and then present important details.
2. I am learning how to identify specific evidence in the text to support my claim and justify my thinking with a triad.	2a. I can highlight textual evidence on the list that reinforces the claim. 2b. I can provide a rationale for why my evidence supports my claim.	2a. Identifying evidence helps you back up or justify your claim. 2b. When you use accurate evidence to support your claim, you become a stronger writer and speaker on a text.	2. Listen to students justify and explain their reasoning in their triads.
3. I am learning how to explain how the evidence supports my claim using the frame "I believe ____ because the text says ____." I am also learning how to use transitional phrases (e.g., for example, for instance, specifically).	3. I can summarize in writing how explicit textual evidence supports my claim.	3. These short draft summaries will be useful when you write your literary analysis essay.	3a. Students connect their evidence to their claim by writing complete sentences in their writing journals to form paragraphs. 3b. Students submit exit slips for teacher to review. Follow up with students who have demonstrated difficulty with this concept.

GUIDED PRACTICE

For your first task in this module, read each learning intention and the potential assessment opportunities that follow. Identify which of the assessments you believe would be most effective for students to engage with the content. In this case, there is no wrong answer. Select one of the two and identify why you believe it would be effective.

LEARNING INTENTION	ASSESSMENT OPPORTUNITY	WHICH ASSESSMENT? WHY?
I am learning how to partition shapes into parts with equal areas.	1. Use dry erase boards with partitioned shapes to hold up for peers and the teacher to check. 2. Use pattern blocks to demonstrate partitioning shapes equally.	
I am learning how to identify reliable and trustworthy content from the Internet.	1. Given a rubric and several websites, including fake websites (e.g., Pacific Northwest Octopus), students identify the reliability and trustworthiness of each. 2. Students analyze websites that they are using in their research, using the criteria for trustworthiness.	
I am learning how to ask questions about unknown words in a text.	1. Discuss the words a student has circled in the text and the questions about the word that the student has written. 2. During a shared reading, students are invited to ask questions about words they do not know.	

CONTINUED

LEARNING INTENTION	ASSESSMENT OPPORTUNITY	WHICH ASSESSMENT? WHY?
I am learning how to identify the impact of water pollution on the environment.	1. Use a practice test to determine areas of mastery and areas of continued instructional need. 2. Summarize the impact in writing using targeted vocabulary and appropriate sentence frames.	
I am learning how to describe how artists use tints and shades in painting.	1. Listen in on partner conversations as students discuss the artists' choices. 2. Given a painting, students analyze the piece in writing, attending to tints and shades.	
I am learning how to predict the resulting geological features resulting from specific plate boundaries (subduction zones, divergent margins, and transform margins).	1. After watching a video of a specific plate boundary, students predict the geological features before the video answers the question. 2. Use a practice test to determine areas of mastery and areas of continued instructional need.	

Note: For suggested answers, please turn to page 133 or visit the companion website at **resources.corwin.com/teacherclarityplaybook**.

For your second task, review the learning intentions from the last unit and identify potential assessment opportunities for checking for understanding.

EXAMPLES	POTENTIAL ASSESSMENT OPPORTUNITIES
Kindergarten: Language Arts **Content learning intention:** I am learning to identify the important events after hearing a story. **Language learning intention:** I am learning to retell the story and include at least three events.	
Grade 1: Math **Content learning intention:** I am learning about how many tens and ones are in a set. **Language learning intention:** I am learning to apply the sentence frame "___ sets of ten and ___ones equal ___." (Ex: "Three sets of ten and 2 ones equal 32.")	
Grade 2: Life Science **Content learning intention:** I am learning to compare and contrast the life cycles. **Language learning intention:** I am learning to summarize the similarities and differences between the life cycle of a frog and a butterfly.	
Grade 3: Language Arts **Content learning intention:** I am learning to evaluate key features of common texts. **Language learning intention:** I am learning to justify why a passage is poetry, fiction, or nonfiction.	
Grade 4: Earth Science **Content learning intention:** I am learning to recognize how landslides, volcanic eruptions, and earthquakes cause changes to rocks. **Language learning intention:** I am learning to use technical vocabulary to discuss how rocks reflect the processes that formed them.	

CONTINUED

CONTINUED

Grade 5: Social Studies **Content learning intention:** I am learning to analyze the major causes of the American Revolution. **Language learning intention:** I am learning to apply compare/contrast signal words in a written explanation the major causes of the American Revolution.	
Grade 6: Math **Content:** I am learning to differentiate between relevant and irrelevant information in word problems. **Language learning intention:** I am learning to explain which aspects of a word problem are relevant and irrelevant.	

Note: For suggested answers, please turn to page 134 or visit the companion website at **resources.corwin.com/teacherclarityplaybook**.

INDEPENDENT PRACTICE

Complete the following template, including assessment opportunities.

STANDARD(S)			

CONCEPTS (NOUNS)		SKILLS (VERBS)	

LEARNING PROGRESSION			

LEARNING INTENTIONS	SUCCESS CRITERIA	TALKING POINTS ON RELEVANCE	ASSESSMENT OPPORTUNITIES

WATCH!

Videos and viewing guide may also be accessed at **resources.corwin.com/teacherclaritplaybook**

VIDEO 7.2
Module 7 in Action—Elementary
resources.corwin.com/teacherclaritplaybook

VIDEO 7.3
Module 7 in Action—Secondary
resources.corwin.com/teacherclaritplaybook

NOTES

_____

_____

_____

_____

_____

_____

_____

_____

_____

_____

_____

_____

_____

_____

_____

_____

_____

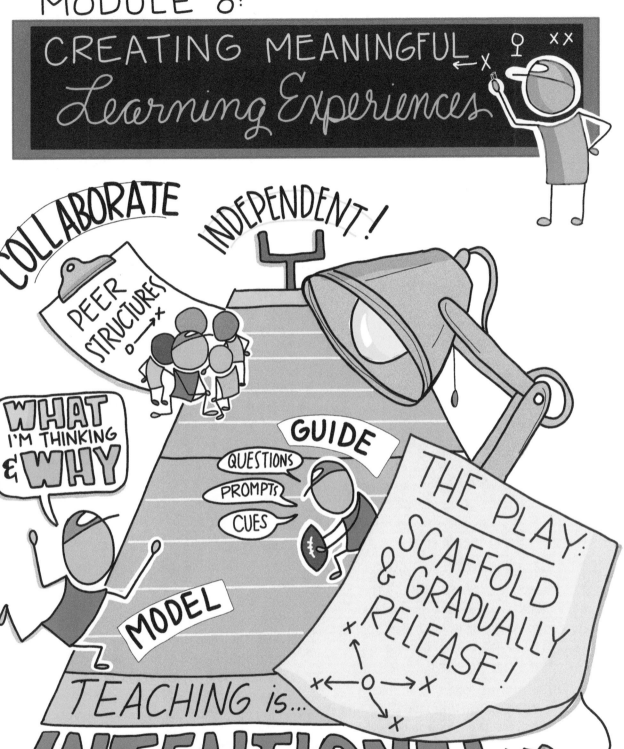

MODULE 8: CREATING MEANINGFUL LEARNING EXPERIENCES

◄ **VIDEO 8.1 Module 8 Overview**
resources.corwin.com/teacherclarityplaybook

Once the learning intentions, success criteria, relevance, and assessment opportunities have been decided upon, it's time to focus on the experiences that will likely provide students with access to the content. This is not simply a random collection of instructional strategies, but rather an intentional set of moves that the teacher makes to scaffold students' learning.

Intentional instruction provides students with access to rigorous learning experiences and can deepen their comprehension and expand their knowledge. One framework that allows for the implementation of intentional instruction is known as gradual release of responsibility (Fisher & Frey, 2014). We think of the phases of gradual release of responsibility, which can be presented in any order that makes sense to meet the learning intentions, as access points.

- *The first access point is teacher modeling of critical thinking.* This method includes the use of think-alouds, worked examples, and other approaches that provide students access to the thinking of an "expert."

- *The second access point is achieved through guided instruction.* Use robust questions, prompts, and cues to scaffold understanding and provide students with the teacher-supported experiences they need to learn.

- *The third access point is collaborative learning.* These peer-led learning experiences require tasks that encourage students to interact with one

another in order to develop a deeper understanding of what they are learning.

- *The fourth access point is independent learning.* Students apply what they have learned as they individually read and write increasingly complex texts.

TEACHER MODELING AND THINKING ALOUD

Effective modeling includes an explanation of why the teacher is doing *what* he or she is doing so that students understand *how* the teacher was able to think, not just *what* the teacher was thinking. When teachers explain their expert thinking in ways that students can understand, students are better able to imitate the thinking of their teachers. We're not looking for students to simply replicate the work of the teacher but rather to explore the ways that other people think. Thinking is invisible, so teachers have to talk about their thinking. By listening to a teacher think, students are supported through the same cognitive processes that the expert uses, as if they were apprentices. Teachers who open up their minds to describe their cognitive and metacognitive processes use a narration process called *think-alouds* (Davey, 1983).

Think-alouds use "I" statements. They activate the ability—some call it an *instinct*—of humans to learn by imitation. Use written notes about your think-aloud that include the word *because*. It's important to explain *why* you're thinking what you're thinking. If not, students experience an example but do not know how to do this on their own. Using *because* reduces the chance that students will be left wondering how you knew to do something or why you think a certain way.

For example, while modeling the comprehension strategy of predicting, you might say, "I can make the following prediction [insert the prediction] because the author told me . . ." Including the *why* while modeling increases the chance that students will be able to imitate the expert thinking they have witnessed because they are provided with examples and the reasons for those examples. Thinking about your thinking is a metacognitive act, and students in turn will start to think more metacognitively when they hear others do so.

GUIDED INSTRUCTION

During guided instruction, teachers provide students just enough support to let them find the answer. The heart of guided instruction is the strategic use of questions to check for understanding, prompts to trigger cognitive and metacognitive thinking, and cues as needed to shift attention more overtly. The teacher provides support by attending to the misconceptions and errors that students make and assisting them in resolving their confusions, rather than simply correcting mistakes.

ASK ROBUST QUESTIONS

Guided instruction begins when the teacher poses a question to check for understanding. The purpose is to uncover potential misconceptions or errors. Ask literal-level questions to check for factual knowledge, but move as quickly as possible to inferential-level questions that require students to synthesize information, speculate, offer opinions, or evaluate information. Then, listen closely to the response with a silent inquiry of your own: *What might this student know and not know at this moment in time that would lead him or her to this response?*

PROMPT FOR COGNITIVE OR METACOGNITIVE WORK

When errors or misconceptions are identified, the first step in resolving them is to prompt the student to engage in mental work, either cognitive or metacognitive. Resist the urge to give them corrective feedback. You might prompt students' use of the following:

- *Background knowledge:* As part of a science passage about the water

cycle, the teacher says, "What do you remember about states of matter?"

- *A process or procedure:* When the student has difficulty starting to develop a writing outline, the teacher says, "I'm thinking about the mnemonic we've used for organizing an explanatory article."

- *Reflective thinking:* The student has just read something incorrectly and the teacher says, "Does that make sense? Really think about it carefully."

CUE TO SHIFT ATTENTION

If prompts fail to resolve the error or misconception, teachers can assume a more directive role through the use of cues. Cues should shift students' attention to something they've missed or overlooked. A simple cue might be, "Take a look at the figure on page 112. Does that help?"

DIRECT EXPLANATIONS

Sometimes, prompts and cues do not resolve errors or misconceptions. In those cases, students cannot be left hanging. Direct explanations should come after prompts and cues to increase the likelihood that students can connect this new information to the knowledge they were using but confusing. Following the direct explanation, the teacher should monitor students' understanding by telling them, "Now, you try it."

COLLABORATIVE LEARNING

Collaborative learning is a critical linchpin in every lesson because it allows students to consolidate their understanding with peers. These small-group (2–5 members), peer-assisted learning opportunities furnish them with a means of applying the skills and strategies learned during modeling and guided instruction. But teachers must structure the time students have to interact with their peers to deepen their knowledge. Examples of collaborative learning structures include the following:

- *Think–pair–share:* Student partners briefly work together to answer a question.

- *Opinion corners:* Students confront a statement and migrate to a labeled corner of the room that reflects their thinking (Strongly Agree/Agree/ Disagree/Strongly Disagree); then, they interact within and across groups.

- *Gallery walks:* Small groups of students visit learning stations to discuss what they are seeing and observing.

- *Literature circles:* Small groups are formed based on interest in a particular book, and they remain together until the book is finished.

- *Jigsaw:* Home and expert groups interact with extended text and one another to learn the content together.

- *Reciprocal teaching:* Four students work with a piece of text using specific comprehension strategies: predicting, questioning, summarizing, and clarifying.

INDEPENDENT LEARNING

Teachers aim to develop a set of skills in each learner that ultimately can be used outside the presence of the teacher. As such, they assign tasks for students to complete both inside the classroom and outside. Independent learning tasks should allow students to practice and apply what they have been taught. This is not the time to introduce new skills or concepts but rather is the time to allow to students an opportunity to demonstrate their understanding.

When instruction is intentional, meaning that the tasks, activities, and assignments are directly linked with learning intentions and success criteria, students have a better chance of learning. It really is that simple. Of course, figuring out all of the components takes time, but it is worth the effort. Student learning is our goal, and there are clear pathways to ensure that students learn *more* and *better* as a result of the experiences they have.

PLC CONVERSATIONS

1. What challenged you in this module?

2. Which of these areas are our collective strengths? How can we develop our skill set in all phases of instruction?

3. How can we match instructional routines and strategies to the learning intentions?

MODELING

The following four examples include suggested activities for teacher modeling, guided and scaffolded instruction, collaborative learning, and independent learning.

GRADE 1: MATH

STANDARD(S)

Solve word problems that call for addition of three whole numbers whose sum is less than or equal to 20 (e.g., by using objects, drawings, and equations with a symbol for the unknown number to represent the problem).

LEARNING INTENTION FOR THIS LESSON:

I am learning how to use the number sentences to restate the problem and make sure it matches. *Use the correct operation words (e.g., plus, add, minus, subtract, equals).*

SUCCESS CRITERIA FOR THIS LESSON

1. I can tell the problem in my own words starting from my number sentence.

2. I can show where the parts of my number sentence are in my model and my picture.

TALKING POINTS ON RELEVANCE

1. Mathematicians use numbers and symbols, not just words.

2. It's easier to add when we see the number and not just the words.

3. It helps us check our answers to see if we are right.

MODEL (STRATEGIES/SKILLS/CONCEPTS TO EMPHASIZE)

1. Read the problem frame aloud to students: "A box of toys was in the room. There were ____ Legos, ____ ball(s), and ____ doll(s). How many toys were in the box?"

2. Roll the dice to fill in each blank, thinking aloud about the number and how to write it.

3. Annotate the problem while thinking aloud about the task and operations.

4. Work through the problem and check for errors.

5. Roll the dice again and fill in new numbers.

6. Continue with several examples, thinking aloud about creating a number sentence and solving the problem.

CONTINUED

GUIDE AND SCAFFOLD

1. Using the same problem frame, invite students to share the pen and update the blanks and then create number sentences.

2. Ask questions that guide students' thinking (e.g., Does the answer make sense? How do you know how many toys there are? How do you know how many balls there are? Which operation do we use?).

3. Visit groups as they work collaboratively and notice errors. Continue to provide prompts and cues for students as they work with their peers.

4. Meet with Stephanie, Horacio, and Mason to check their limited understanding based on the previous lesson.

5. Meet with Alfredo, Quan, Huda, and Carla and have them create a new number problem given their high level of performance on the previous lesson.

COLLABORATIVE LEARNING

1. Provide students a new problem frame printed on laminated paper: "A basket of fruit is on the table. The basket has ____ apple(s), ____ orange(s), and ____ pear(s). How many pieces of fruit all together?"

2. Read the problem aloud to ensure that students know all of the words.

3. Provide each group with a dry erase marker, eraser, and die.

4. Students roll the die and fill in the numbers. One student (rotating) reads the statement, and the peers offer a thumbs-up or thumbs-down. If thumbs-down, the peers provide feedback.

5. The students write a number sentence on their dry erase boards and then compare answers.

6. The students use sentence frames to agree and disagree with each other.

7. Students write out the answer to the problem using a complete sentence and then compare their responses.

INDEPENDENT LEARNING

1. Students are provided three problems to glue into their math journals, and they solve these problems independently.

2. Students write out the answer to the problems in complete sentences (e.g., There are 12 tools in the box.).

ASSESSMENT OPPORTUNITIES

1. Use number and operation cards to build their sentences.

2. Use sentence strips for students to write their equations in long form.

STANDARD(S)

Determine the main idea of a text and explain how it is supported by key details; summarize the text.

LEARNING INTENTION FOR THIS LESSON

I am learning to establish the relative importance of ideas and details presented in the text and share my thinking with peers in complete sentences.

SUCCESS CRITERIA FOR THIS LESSON

1. I can rate the ideas and details in terms of their importance from low to high.

2. I can explain the importance of the ideas and details that have been selected.

TALKING POINTS ON RELEVANCE

1. Knowing the difference between interesting ideas and important details helps you find the main idea.

2. Collecting interesting ideas and important details are useful when you write about a reading.

MODEL (STRATEGIES/SKILLS/CONCEPTS TO EMPHASIZE)

1. Model and think aloud using an informational text about butterflies.

2. Underline each idea and detail while students do the same.

3. Read the text a second time, catching a detail that was missed on the first read.

4. Then, rank the ideas/details in importance.

5. For each idea/detail, think aloud about how valuable it is and then rate it on a scale of 1 to 5 in importance.

6. Review the list and focus on the ideas that are very important, thinking aloud about the information.

CONTINUED

GUIDE AND SCAFFOLD

1. How do I know if it is a detail?

2. How do I know if a detail or idea is important?

3. Which idea is more important, given what you know about the text?

Notice students who have not underlined ideas or details and provide additional prompting.

Notice students who are not providing reasons for their selections or rankings and provide additional guidance.

Meet with James, Brian, Tran, and Alexandria when groups begin to focus on the concept of details and ideas, which were not solid, based on their previous performance data.

COLLABORATIVE LEARNING

Students glue the text about frogs into their writing journals. They read the first paragraph, identifying details and ideas. They discuss with their assigned partner, providing reasons for their selections. Then, they continue through the text, discussing each paragraph with a partner. Next, they rank the ideas on a scale of 1 to 5, discussing their rankings with peers and providing reasons for their rankings.

INDEPENDENT LEARNING

Students summarize the most important details and ideas, based on their rankings, in their journals.

ASSESSMENT OPPORTUNITIES

In their writing journals, students rank the ideas and details from lowest to highest and include a written rationale for the order they have identified. Listen in on partner conversations as students discuss their ratings.

GRADE 8: MATH

STANDARD(S)

Know and apply the properties of integer exponents to generate equivalent numerical expressions.

LEARNING INTENTION FOR THIS LESSON

I am learning to discover the product property of exponents by expanding and simplifying exponential expressions. *Accurately identify the base and exponent of exponential terms.*

SUCCESS CRITERIA FOR THIS LESSON

1a. I can expand exponential expressions.

1b. I can simplify multiplication strings by using exponential notation.

1c. I can write a rule for multiplying two powers with the same base.

TALKING POINTS ON RELEVANCE

1a. Exponential notation allows us to denote complicated quantities in a simpler way.

1b. The product property is a tool that mathematicians use to make very large calculations much simpler.

MODEL (STRATEGIES/SKILLS/CONCEPTS TO EMPHASIZE)

Model for students how to expand exponential expressions and show how emphasizing the academic language *base* and *exponent* guides this process (e.g., *Consider x^5. Since my base is x and my exponent is 5, this means x times itself 5 times, or, x·x·x·x·x.*). For the sake of discovery, limit initial teacher modeling solely to this basic tool.

GUIDE AND SCAFFOLD

1. How can we use what we learned about expanding exponential expressions to simplify repeated multiplication (e.g., How can we simplify $y·y·y·y·y·y$)? Remember, anything that can be done *forward* in math can be done *backward*.

2. How can we bring these two tools (expanding and simplifying) together to rewrite a product of powers (e.g., How can we *expand* and then *simplify* $z^4·z^9$)?

Students who are struggling to get started should be offered additional focusing and/or funneling questions. If that does not work, prompt and cue. Teacher modeling can always be revisited as an ultimate scaffold for access.

COLLABORATIVE LEARNING

Students complete a task in their assigned groups whereby they seek to find a pattern (the product property) by generating data from their work on a problem set. Handouts are provided, but the work is completed in students' math notebooks for accountability and assessment. In addition to showing their work for expanding and simplifying products of exponential expressions, students will record initial exponent values for each term being multiplied *and* the single resulting exponential value [e.g., $a^3·a^6 = (a·a·a) · (a·a·a·a·a·a) = a^9$. Initial exponent values: 3, 6. Resulting exponent value: 9]. Students will discuss this data to write and justify a rule for multiplying two powers with the same base.

CONTINUED

INDEPENDENT LEARNING

Students summarize their learning experience in their math notebooks by writing a rule for the product of powers, explaining what it means, and by providing a novel example that justifies their claim.

ASSESSMENT OPPORTUNITIES

1a. Listen as groups work through the task. Are students accurately identifying the base and exponent of exponential terms?

1b. Students record their work for the task in their math notebooks. Are they properly expanding and simplifying exponential expressions?

1c. Culminate the day with a whole-class discussion describing the patterns students noticed. Can they write the product property as a rule from their experience?

GRADE 10: ELA

STANDARD(S)

Cite strong and thorough textual evidence to support analysis of what the text says explicitly as well as inferences drawn from the text.

LEARNING INTENTION FOR THIS LESSON

I am learning to identify specific evidence in the text to support your claim. *Justify your thinking with a triad.*

SUCCESS CRITERIA FOR THIS LESSON

1. I can highlight textual evidence on the list that reinforces the claim.

2. I can provide a rationale for why my evidence supports my claim.

TALKING POINTS ON RELEVANCE

1. Identifying evidence helps you back up or justify your claim.

2. When you use accurate evidence to support your claim, you become a stronger writer and speaker on a text.

Post these sentence frames for all students throughout the lesson to support discussion: Does this evidence prove or support my claim? How does this evidence prove or support my claim?

- X states, "___."

- According to X, "___."

- In X's view, "___."

- X agrees when she writes, "___."

- X disagrees when he writes, "___."

Explaining quotations:

- Basically, X is warning/saying ___.

- In other words, X believes ___.

- In making this comment, X urges us to ___.

- X's point is that ___.

- The essence of X's argument is that ___. (Graff & Birkenstein, 2014)

Model how you are thinking about your claim, specifically what your claim means. So that all students can see, use a graphic organizer to model what you must prove or support. Once you have identified what you must prove or support, use the text to highlight or underline evidence that does just that. Add the evidence to your graphic organizer so that you can begin to support your claim. Model how you use the sentence frames to write complete sentences using the evidence. Do this two times so that students can visually see you while listening to you find evidence to prove/support your claim.

Pose/answer these questions: **Does** this evidence prove or support my claim? **How** does this evidence prove or support my claim?

CONTINUED

GUIDE AND SCAFFOLD

Ask students to work in partners to find one more piece of evidence from the text to prove or support their claim while using a frame to write it in their journals. Students share their findings at their tables and select one partnership to share with the whole class.

Discussion questions for the large group:

Does this evidence prove or support the claim?

How does this evidence prove or support the claim?

Write a complete sentence using their evidence and one of the frames.

Listen in to partnerships. Prompt and cue as needed. Redirect attention to your modeling samples when needed.

Identify any students who will need additional support in a teacher-directed small group.

COLLABORATIVE LEARNING

Provide a claim based on a familiar text to groups of three. Each student must have access to the text.

Students must identify three pieces of evidence from the text to prove or support the claim.

Students should use the frames as supports when writing the evidence in complete sentences.

Each triad will post its evidence on a chart for a gallery walk.

During the gallery walk, students should evaluate the effectiveness and appropriateness of the evidence used to prove or support the claim.

INDEPENDENT LEARNING

Students use their own text to find evidence to prove or support their individual claim(s).

They should begin to build their graphic organizers, use the frames provided, and refer to the teacher and peer examples.

ASSESSMENT OPPORTUNITIES

Listen to students working collaboratively as they find evidence that proves or supports their claim.

Read student charts in the gallery walk to assess effectiveness and language.

Identify small groups to pull for additional support during independent learning time.

Observe student body language during modeling, collaborative, and independent learning opportunities.

GUIDED PRACTICE

For your first task, review each learning intention and the assessment opportunity. Describe how you could engage students in the targeted access point in the third column as part of a lesson. Of course, each lesson would have all access points, but we're just practicing here.

LEARNING INTENTION	ASSESSMENT OPPORTUNITY	MEANINGFUL INSTRUCTION
I am learning to partition shapes into parts with equal areas.	Use pattern blocks to demonstrate partitioning shapes equally.	Collaborative:
I am learning to identify reliable and trustworthy content from the Internet.	Given a rubric and several websites, including fake websites (e.g., Pacific Northwest Octopus), students identify the reliability and trustworthiness of each.	Modeling:
I am learning to ask questions about unknown words in a text.	During a shared reading, students are invited to ask questions about words they do not know.	Modeling:
I am learning to identify the impact of water pollution on the environment.	Summarize the impact in writing using targeted vocabulary and appropriate sentence frames.	Independent:
I am learning to describe how artists use tints and shades in painting.	Listen in on partner conversations as students discuss the artists' choices.	Collaborative:

CONTINUED

LEARNING INTENTION	ASSESSMENT OPPORTUNITY	MEANINGFUL INSTRUCTION
I am learning to predict resulting geological features, given a specific plate boundary (subduction zones, divergent margins, and transform margins).	After watching a video of a specific plate boundary, students predict the geological features before the video answers the question.	Guided:

Note: For suggested answers, please turn to page 135 or visit the companion website at **resources. corwin.com/teacherclarityplaybook**.

For your second task, revisit the previous learning intentions and identify one type of instruction required for students to master the learning intention. This could be focused instruction, guided instruction, collaborative learning opportunities, or independent learning.

EXAMPLES	IDEAS FOR MEANINGFUL INSTRUCTION
Kindergarten: Language Arts **Content learning intention:** I am learning to identify the important events after hearing a story. **Language learning intention:** I am learning to retell the story and include at least three events.	
Grade 1: Math **Content learning intention:** I am learning about how many tens and ones are in a set. **Language learning intention:** I am learning to apply the sentence frame "___ sets of ten and ___ ones equal ___." (Ex: "Three sets of ten and 2 ones equal 32.")	
Grade 2: Life Science **Content learning intention:** I am learning to compare and contrast the life cycles. **Language learning intention:** I am learning to summarize the similarities and differences between the life cycle of a frog and a butterfly.	

EXAMPLES	IDEAS FOR MEANINGFUL INSTRUCTION
Grade 3: Language Arts **Content learning intention:** I am learning to evaluate key features of common texts. **Language learning intention:** I am learning to justify why a passage is poetry, fiction, or nonfiction.	
Grade 4: Earth Science **Content learning intention:** I am learning to recognize how landslides, volcanic eruptions, and earthquakes cause changes to rocks. **Language learning intention:** I am learning to use technical vocabulary to discuss how rocks reflect the processes that formed them.	
Grade 5: Social Studies **Content learning intention:** I am learning to analyze the major causes of the American Revolution. **Language learning intention:** I am learning to apply compare/contrast signal words in a written explanation the major causes of the American Revolution.	
Grade 6: Math **Content:** I am learning to differentiate between relevant and irrelevant information in word problems. **Language learning intention:** I am learning to explain which aspects of a word problem are relevant and irrelevant.	

Note: For suggested answers, please turn to page 136 or visit the companion website at **resources .corwin.com/teacherclarityplaybook**.

INDEPENDENT PRACTICE

Choose your own standard and fill in the template, including the new section on the activities you would use for each type of instruction.

STANDARD(S)

LEARNING INTENTION FOR THIS LESSON

SUCCESS CRITERIA FOR THIS LESSON

TALKING POINTS ON RELEVANCE

MODEL (STRATEGIES/SKILLS/CONCEPTS TO EMPHASIZE)

GUIDE AND SCAFFOLD

COLLABORATIVE LEARNING

INDEPENDENT LEARNING

ASSESSMENT OPPORTUNITIES

For a blank version of the independent practice pages in this book, visit **resources.corwin.com/teacherclarityplaybook**

WATCH!

Videos and viewing guide may also be accessed at **resources.corwin.com/teacherclarityplaybook**

VIDEO 8.2
Module 8 in Action—Elementary
resources.corwin.com/teacherclarityplaybook

VIDEO 8.3
Module 8 in Action—Secondary
resources.corwin.com/teacherclarityplaybook

NOTES

_____

_____

_____

_____

_____

_____

_____

_____

_____

_____

_____

_____

_____

_____

_____

_____

_____

_____

NOTES

MODULE 9: ESTABLISHING MASTERY OF STANDARDS

◀ VIDEO 9.1 Module 9 Overview
resources.corwin.com/teacherclarityplaybook

Summative assessment is the link between teaching and learning. It is not sufficient to say that by virtue of the fact that we have taught something, students have learned it. On the other hand, it is also unacceptable to blame students for *not* learning. Summative assessments give students information about their learning, and they give teachers feedback about their teaching.

PURPOSES OF SUMMATIVE ASSESSMENTS

End-of-unit and end-of-course assessments are used for awarding grades and reporting achievement on report cards and transcripts. In addition, they provide information about the knowledge and skills acquired by the student. Summative assessments include tests, projects, writing assignments, and performances. As noted previously, assessment should occur throughout the unit (formatively), not just at the end. However, end-of-unit summative assessments are important because they provide a measure of student performance against an exemplar—the standard. These are sometimes referred to as criterion-referenced assessments because the criteria for success have been identified. These differ from norm-referenced tests that compare the performance of an individual or group against a larger population. Everyone can theoretically earn an A on criterion-referenced assessments; only a fixed portion of students could do so on a norm-referenced exam. But criterion-referenced assessments have shortcomings, as they are

dependent on how well the standard is written and how well the assessment item measures it. To develop a sound summative assessment that measures the standard, return to the process you used to design your instruction in the first place.

1. **Return to the concepts and skills outlined in the standard.** Reexamine the concepts (nouns) and skills (verbs) featured in the standard. Make sure that they are clearly present in the assessment you are designing.

2. **Let the learning progressions guide your assessment.** Remember all that work you did in figuring out what the learning progressions would be for your unit? Here's where they pay off. The learning progressions, which are the tent poles for instruction, are also the tent poles for assessment. You will recall that the learning progressions are those big-bucket concepts and skills students must acquire to master the standard. The half dozen or so learning progressions you developed for the unit represent key elements of the standard being measured, including underlying background knowledge. Make sure each is represented in your assessment.

3. **Consult your daily learning intentions for further detail.** The learning intentions expand each of the learning progressions into daily statements of purpose for students. While some will be too fine-grained to be of use in your summative assessment, others may stand out in importance. Revisit your learning intentions to see if there are any that would be of use on your assessment.

4. **Refer to success criteria to show students the link between what is being measured and what has been learned.** The success criteria

should guide the item development of the specific assessment tool. Some teachers list success criteria statements directly on the assessment to strengthen ties between mastery and demonstration of learning. Rubrics or checklists used during the unit should be employed on the assessment.

5. **Match language expectations to assessment types.** Your language learning intentions provide direction on the design of the assessment. Student demonstration of mastery in the assessment should be consistent with the ways they did so during the unit of study. The use of writing prompts and exit slips, for instance, means that students should be completing constructed written responses. Performance-based demonstrations of skills during the unit should likewise be assessed through similar channels.

6. **Cross-check for relevance.** Throughout the unit you have made it a point to ensure that students would be able to see the relevance to what they were learning. Ask yourself, has your assessment expressed relevance of learning?

Taken together, this process allows you to determine which students have mastered the standard(s) and which need additional instruction to be successful. This completes the teaching and learning cycle and signals the start of a new unit, as well as potential interventions for students who still need it.

PLC CONVERSATIONS

1. What challenged you in this module?

2. What does it mean to have really learned something at a deep level?

3. What will we do if students do not master the standards?

MODELING

The following are four examples of assessment formats and assessment details that are linked to standard(s), key concepts and skills, learning progressions, and relevancy.

GRADE 1: MATH

STANDARD(S) TO BE ASSESSED

Solve word problems that call for addition of three whole numbers whose sum is less than or equal to 20 (e.g., by using objects, drawings, and equations with a symbol for the unknown number to represent the problem).

KEY CONCEPTS TO BE ASSESSED

Word problem
Addition
Whole numbers
Sum
Objects
Drawings
Equations
Symbol
Unknown number
Problem

KEY SKILLS TO BE ASSESSED

Solve
Use
Represent

LEARNING PROGRESSIONS TO FRAME THE ASSESSMENT

1. Analyze word problems to determine which actions and attributes call for the operation of addition.

2. Analyze word problems to identify whole numbers in the task.

3. Use objects to represent numbers in a word problem and add those objects together.

4. Use drawings to represent numbers in a word problem and add those objects together.

5. Develop an equation to represent the information in the word problem.

6. Use a symbol to represent the unknown number in a word problem.

7. Solve problems that contain three addends in a word problem.

The Teacher Clarity Playbook

ASSESSMENT FORMATS

○ Multiple choice items

○ Dichotomous choice items

✓ Short, constructed response items

○ Extended essay revsponse

○ Culminating individual project

○ Culminating group project

○ Performance

○ Portfolio or exhibition

RELEVANCY CHECK: DOES THIS ASSESSMENT DEMONSTRATE . . .

✓ Relevancy outside the classroom?

○ Relevancy co-constructed with students?

○ Learning about oneself as a learner?

✓ Relevancy within the discipline?

ASSESSMENT DETAILS

The primary assessment for this standard is word problems. The task of converting words into mathematical operations is an important one for young children to master. As noted in the standard, students need to demonstrate multiple ways for demonstrating their knowledge, including using objects and drawings, as well as constructing mathematical equations.

Annabelle brought fresh fruit from her family's trees to share with her class. She brought 7 avocados, 4 oranges, and 8 guavas. How many pieces of fruit did Annabelle have in all?

Draw it: _____ _____ _____

Add math signs: _____ ☐ _____ ☐ _____ ☐ _____

Write a math equation: _____

STANDARD(S) TO BE ASSESSED

Determine the main idea of a text and explain how it is supported by key details; summarize the text.

KEY CONCEPTS TO BE ASSESSED

Main idea
Key details
Text

KEY SKILLS TO BE ASSESSED

Determine
Explain
Summarize

LEARNING PROGRESSIONS TO FRAME THE ASSESSMENT

1   Identify at least three details in an informational text.

2   Recognize the central or main idea when the author provides a topic sentence.

3   Determine the central or main idea when the author does not provide a topic sentence.

4   Using the main idea and details, summarize the information provided in the text.

5   Explain how the details in a text support the central or main idea.

ASSESSMENT FORMATS

o Multiple choice items

o Dichotomous choice items

o Short, constructed response items

✓ Extended essay response

✓ Culminating individual project

o Culminating group project

✓ Performance

o Portfolio or exhibition

RELEVANCY CHECK: *DOES THIS ASSESSMENT DEMONSTRATE . . .*

✓ Relevancy outside the classroom?

o Relevancy co-constructed with students?

✓ Learning about oneself as a learner?

✓ Relevancy within the discipline?

ASSESSMENT DETAILS

The standard could be assessed though a written response to a prompt using an informational article read and discussed in class. When using a writing prompt, it is important to provide clear and coherent directions in order to obtain desired responses. Here is a suggested writing prompt for this standard:

How does it work? After reading an informational article about _____, write an explanatory essay in which you 1) summarize the main idea from the article,

2) provide important details from the text to support the main idea, and 3) explain how the details you selected support the main idea.

Alternatively, students could deliver a short oral report to the class on an informational book they have read about a topic under study in science or social studies. The presentation would include the title of the resource and a summary of the major points and supporting details.

A third option would be for students to write online book reviews explaining the informational text they read and furnishing the main idea and key supporting details cited in the book.

GRADE 8: MATH

STANDARD(S) TO BE ASSESSED
Know and apply the properties of integer exponents to generate equivalent numerical expressions.

KEY CONCEPTS TO BE ASSESSED
Properties of integer exponents
Equivalent numerical expressions

KEY SKILLS TO BE ASSESSED
Know
Apply
Generate

LEARNING PROGRESSIONS TO FRAME THE ASSESSMENT

1   Discover and use the product and quotient properties of exponents.

2   Discover and use the meaning of an exponent of 0.

3   Define negative exponents and use them to rewrite exponential expressions.

4   Discover and use the power to a power property of exponents.

5   Generate equivalent expressions by applying multiple properties of exponents.

ASSESSMENT FORMATS
✓ Multiple choice items

o Dichotomous choice items

✓ Short, constructed response items

o Extended essay response

o Culminating individual project

✓ Culminating group project

o Performance

o Portfolio or exhibition

RELEVANCY CHECK: *DOES THIS ASSESSMENT DEMONSTRATE . . .*
o Relevancy outside the classroom?

o Relevancy co-constructed with students?

o Relevancy based on learning about oneself as a learner?

✓ Relevancy within the discipline?

ASSESSMENT DETAILS

This standard lends itself to an array of assessment opportunities and modalities. One such example from a test to be administered on a laptop is provided here.

Which of the following numerical expressions are equivalent to 7^6? Check all that apply.

[a] 7^{-6}	[b] $\dfrac{1}{7^{-6}}$	[c] $\dfrac{1}{7^6}$	[d] $7^2 \cdot 7^3$
[e] $7^3 \cdot 7^3$	[f] $(7^3)^3$	[g] $(7^3)^2$	[h] $\dfrac{7^{12}}{7 \cdot 7^5}$

Notice in this "Check all that apply"-style item, students will need to use various properties of exponents in order to assess the equivalence of *each* option. The inherent benefit for the teacher is the targeted data generated about the specific level of mastery the student has met toward the standard.

Another means of assessing this standard is through a collaborative group task.

TASK: 1 = . . . ?
Create an expression equivalent to "1" using at least five different bases and *each* property of exponents at least once.

This type of task elicits conversation and self-regulation amongst peers. *Have we used five bases? Have we used each property of exponents? (What are all the properties of exponents?) Does our expression equal 1?* The increased rigor of a task such as this warrants the collaborative delivery as a scaffold for access. Students now have the opportunity to collectively *make sense of problems* and collaboratively *persevere in solving them* (Standard for Mathematical Practice 1). The goal post of the task is to *construct a viable argument*—through which students will be *critiquing* their own *reasoning* and the reasoning of their fellow group members (Standard for Mathematical Practice 3). And simply by virtue of being a task that requires discussion, students can exercise their *attention to precision* (Standard for Mathematical Practice 6) in their communication with peers. This is an example of using a content standard as a delivery vehicle for the practice standards.

GRADE 10: ENGLISH

STANDARD(S) TO BE ASSESSED
Cite strong and thorough textual evidence to support analysis of what the text says explicitly as well as inferences drawn from the text.

KEY CONCEPTS TO BE ASSESSED
Textual evidence

Analysis of explicit text

Analysis of inferences

KEY SKILLS TO BE ASSESSED
Cite

Support

Draw from

LEARNING PROGRESSIONS TO FRAME THE ASSESSMENT

1. Determine the major themes, plot, characters, and setting of the text.

2. Make inferences about the text.

3. Create a logical claim based on the text.

4. Use evidence to support an analysis of what the text explicitly says.

5. Use evidence to support inferences drawn from the text.

6. Use formal reasoning to explain how the evidence supports your claim.

7. Use MLA format for citations.

ASSESSMENT FORMATS

- ○ Multiple choice items
- ○ Dichotomous choice items
- ○ Short, constructed response items
- ✓ Extended essay response

- ○ Culminating individual project
- ○ Culminating group project
- ○ Performance
- ○ Portfolio or exhibition

RELEVANCY CHECK: *DOES THIS ASSESSMENT DEMONSTRATE . . .*
- ○ Relevancy outside the classroom?
- ✓ Relevancy co-constructed with students?
- ✓ Learning about oneself as a learner?
- ✓ Relevancy within the discipline?

ASSESSMENT DETAILS

This standard necessarily requires that the skill be demonstrated through writing and builds from the short, constructed responses and exit tickets they have completed throughout the unit.

The writing prompt should be clearly stated to elicit the desired response. It should contain specifics about the success criteria and should be linked to the standard and its relevancy. This can be achieved through an organizing question.

Writing Prompt: What makes a story effective for its purpose? After reading _____, write a 350 to 500 word essay that includes a coherent claim supported by at least six examples of textual evidence cited from the text. Evidence must include three explicit and three inferential items, including reasoning to support your claim. Be sure to accurately cite using MLA format.

The task demand for this standard may vary and can include one of several possibilities:

- Students are given a new short story to read, annotate, and analyze on their own a week before the summative assessment.
- Students apply the concepts and skills learned in this unit of study to analyze their own independent reading selection.
- Students apply the concepts and skills learned in this unit of study to analyze an assigned reading selection from the unit of study.
- Students apply the concepts and skills learned in this unit of study by watching and then analyzing a short multimedia text.

GUIDED PRACTICE

For your first task, we have included a range of social studies and science standards. For each standard, we have identified ways that the standard might be assessed. Identify items for each that would allow teachers to determine student mastery of the content.

STANDARD	ASSESSMENT FORMAT	SAMPLE ITEMS OR TASKS FOR ASSESSMENT
Identify geographical features in their local region (e.g., deserts, mountains, valleys, hills, coastal areas, oceans, lakes). (Grade 3, CA)	Culminating group project	
Understand the relationship between religion and the social and political order in Mesopotamia and Egypt. (Grade 6, CA)	Multiple choice and dichotomous choice items	
Explain how the ideology of the French Revolution led France to develop from constitutional monarchy to democratic despotism to the Napoleonic empire. (Grade 10, CA)	Short constructed response items	
Make observations to construct an evidence-based account that objects in darkness can be seen only when illuminated. (Grade 1, NCSS)	Culminating individual project	
Identify evidence from patterns in rock formations and fossils in rock layers to support an explanation for changes in a landscape over time. (Grade 4, NGSS)	Performance	

CONTINUED

CONTINUED

STANDARD	ASSESSMENT FORMAT	SAMPLE ITEMS OR TASKS FOR ASSESSMENT
Construct and revise an explanation based on evidence for the cycling of matter and flow of energy in aerobic and anaerobic conditions. (HS, NGSS)	Extended essay response	

Note: For suggested answers, please turn to page 137 or visit the companion website at **resources.corwin.com/teacherclarityplaybook**.

For your second task, review the assessment item and identify which aspects of relevancy the task could address. There may be more than one response for each.

ASSESSMENT ITEM	RELEVANCE CHECK
Complete the essay prompt and on a separate page, identify the writing processes you used.	☐ Relevance outside the classroom ☐ Relevancy co-constructed with students ☐ Relevance based on learning about oneself as a learner ☐ Relevance within the discipline
We have the opportunity to recarpet the classroom, but we need to know the square footage of the room. How many different ways can you identify to figure out the size of the room?	☐ Relevance outside the classroom ☐ Relevancy co-constructed with students ☐ Relevance based on learning about oneself as a learner ☐ Relevance within the discipline
This exam has five parts (multiple choice, true/false, matching, short responses, and fill in the blank). You should complete any two sections that allow you to demonstrate your understanding.	☐ Relevance outside the classroom ☐ Relevancy co-constructed with students ☐ Relevance based on learning about oneself as a learner ☐ Relevance within the discipline
Generate 10 possible exam questions of any format. I will consider all of them as potential questions that allow the class to determine mastery of the content.	☐ Relevance outside the classroom ☐ Relevancy co-constructed with students ☐ Relevance based on learning about oneself as a learner ☐ Relevance within the discipline

ASSESSMENT ITEM	RELEVANCE CHECK
Produce an iMovie in which you retell the content of this unit of study. You should have a narrator and include the technical vocabulary we have learned in this unit.	☐ Relevance outside the classroom ☐ Relevancy co-constructed with students ☐ Relevance based on learning about oneself as a learner ☐ Relevance within the discipline

Note: For suggested answers, please turn to page 139 or visit the companion website at **resources.corwin.com/teacherclarityplaybook**.

INDEGENDENT PRACTICE

Finally, using your own standard, fill in the following template, including assessment formats and details.

STANDARD(S) TO BE ASSESSED:

KEY CONCEPTS TO BE ASSESSED:

KEY SKILLS TO BE ASSESSED:

LEARNING PROGRESSIONS TO FRAME THE ASSESSMENT:

ASSESSMENT FORMATS:

- Multiple choice items
- Dichotomous choice items
- Short, constructed response items
- Extended essay response

- Culminating individual project
- Culminating group project
- Performance
- Portfolio or exhibition

RELEVANCY CHECK: *DOES THIS ASSESSMENT DEMONSTRATE . . .*

- Relevancy outside the classroom?
- Relevancy co-constructed with students?
- Learning about oneself as a learner?
- Relevancy within the discipline?

ASSESSMENT DETAILS:

WATCH!

Videos and viewing guide may also be accessed at **resources.corwin.com/teacherclarityplaybook**

VIDEO 9.2
Module 9 in Action—Elementary
resources.corwin.com/teacherclarityplaybook

VIDEO 9.3
Module 9 in Action—Secondary
resources.corwin.com/teacherclarityplaybook

NOTES

_____

_____

_____

_____

_____

_____

_____

_____

_____

_____

_____

_____

_____

_____

_____

_____

_____

MOVING FORWARD

We made some bold claims at the beginning of this playbook. We suggested that focusing on teacher clarity could revolutionize your practice. To be clear, we don't believe that this is a simple panacea to a complex problem. In fact, each step in the teacher clarity process requires a tremendous amount of thought and reflection. But now that you have worked your way through the process, we hope that you have glimpsed new possibilities. As with any undertaking in education, you need to decide how you will measure your own success. Here are four suggestions.

ASK STUDENTS WHAT THEY ARE LEARNING AND WHY THEY ARE LEARNING IT

While learning intentions and success criteria launch learning, they don't end with your carefully crafted statements of purpose. Ask your students to explain their learning in their own words. They will be hesitant at first—this is new for them, too. But the language of learners can give you great insight into their perceptions and developmental needs.

USE PRE-ASSESSMENT AND POST-ASSESSMENT DATA TO COMPARE RESULTS

Collect data on what students know before the unit begins and compare it to what they know at the end. It doesn't have to be elaborate. Five or ten pre-assessment questions (ungraded, of course) is enough to determine what they gained through your instruction. Without this information, you won't know if students learned anything from you; it may have been that they already knew the content before the lessons.

SHARE RESULTS WITH STUDENTS

Students thrive on data about themselves. Share their gains throughout the unit so they can chart their own progress. No student should have to wait until the summative assessment to figure out whether she or he learned something. It is demotivating when a learner believes it is wholly up to the teacher to determine success. Bring students into the process from the beginning.

COLLABORATE WITH COLLEAGUES

There is a reason teaching is considered both a science and an art—it certainly requires technical skills, but it also needs the inspiration that comes from talking through challenging problems in the company of caring colleagues. Teaching and learning are social endeavors, and they demand that we share our challenges and successes. It is how we cultivate the very best we can be as educators. When you discuss teaching with others, you have the opportunity to influence their practices and improve your own.

Remember, the first question of an effective PLC is this: "Where are we going?" Teams of teachers can use the process outlined in this handbook to determine their answer to that question. Of course, it will involve an analysis of the standards. But as we have seen, developing meaningful learning experiences for students requires more than analyzing the standards. Figuring out what students need to learn involves identifying a learning progression and then the daily learning intentions.

The second question that PLC team members ask is "Where are we now?" Teams work together to identify the needs of their students in terms of language development, and to increase relevancy to engage learners. The third PLC+ question, "How do we move learning forward?" is crucial as teams work collaboratively to identify formative assessment opportunities paired with meaningful instruction.

The final question that PLC+ team members ask is "Who benefited and who did not?" These get to the heart of the equity work that is ongoing as we raise achievement for each student. Once gaps have been identified, teachers intervene. These interventions are based on the learning intentions and success criteria that students did not master, not new content. And when students already know the content, teachers can accelerate and develop alternatives for students.

In sum, teacher clarity is an important area of attention for teachers and one that can result in significant gains in students' learning. But without a clear vision of where we are going, and how we might get there, some students remain at perpetual risk of failure. We owe it to every child we serve to ensure a clear vision of the destination, and a robust plan to make sure that everyone crosses the finish line.

APPENDIX

SUGGESTED ANSWERS TO GUIDED QUESTIONS

Module 1

Suggested Answers

For the following examples, identify the nouns and verbs. First, circle the verbs and underline the nouns; then, place them in the corresponding boxes.

GRADE 7: ELA

STANDARD(S):

(Write) arguments to (support) claims with clear reasons and relevant evidence.

(c) (Use) words, phrases, and clauses to (create) cohesion and (clarify) the relationships among claim(s), reasons, and evidence.

CONCEPTS (NOUNS):	SKILLS (VERBS):
Arguments	Write
Claims	Support
Reasons	Use
Evidence	Create
Words	Qualify
Phrases	
Causes	
Cohesion	
Relationships	
Claims	
Reasons	
Evidence	

STANDARD(S):

(Tell) and (write) time to the nearest <u>minute</u> and (measure) time intervals in <u>minutes</u>. (Solve) <u>word problems</u> involving <u>addition</u> and <u>subtraction</u> of <u>time intervals</u> in <u>minutes</u> (e.g., by (representing) the <u>problem</u> on a <u>number line diagram</u>).

CONCEPTS (NOUNS):	SKILLS (VERBS):
Time	Tell
Minute(s)	Write
Time intervals	Measure
Word problems	Solve
Addition	Represent
Subtraction	
Number line diagram	

Module 2

Suggested Answers

We have written learning progressions for the following eighth-grade social studies standard. For your first task, place the learning progressions in a logical sequence. Put a number 1 next to the one you believe comes first, a number 2 on the next logical progression, and so on.

Ohio Social Studies Standard 21
Grade 8: Roles and Systems of Government
The U.S. Constitution protects citizens' rights by limiting the powers of government.

[3] Describe the role of the U.S. Constitution as a foundational document.

[5] Identify the three branches of the U.S. government.

[1] Explain what is meant by the powers of the government.

[2] Understand the conflict of the framers in balancing states' rights with federal government powers.

[4] Recognize the Bill of Rights' role in limiting the powers of government.

[6] Enumerate the protections provided to U.S. citizens by the Constitution as amended.

For this second task, create a set of learning progressions for the following standard for students in first-grade ELA:

Distinguish shades of meaning among verbs differing in manner (e.g., look, peek, glance, stare, glare, scowl) and adjectives differing in intensity (e.g., large, gigantic, small, tiny) by defining or choosing them or by acting out the meanings.

1. Define related words.

2. Understand and recognize manner in verbs.

3. Understand and recognize intensity in adjectives.

4. Distinguish which phrases achieve desired effects.

5. Explain or act out differences in related words.

6. _____

7. _____

8. _____

Module 3

Suggested Answers

First, identify a logical sequence of **learning intentions** based on the learning progression and standard that follows:

Earth and Space Science (NGSS) HS-ESS2-1 Earth's Systems, Plate Tectonics and Large-Scale

Standard: *System Interactions:*

Plate tectonics is the unifying theory that explains the past and current movements of rocks at Earth's surface and provides a framework for understanding its geologic history.

One in a sequence of learning progressions:

3) There are three types of plate boundaries: subduction zones, divergent margins, and transform margins. Their movement results in various geological features and events.

Number these learning intentions in a logical sequence:

[3] I am learning about the unique movements associated with the three types of plate boundaries.

[5] I am learning about the differences between the types of geological features that result from plate boundaries movement (subduction, divergent, and transform).

[1] I am learning that geologic features result from plate boundary movement.

[2] I am learning about the characteristics of subduction zones, divergent zones, and transform margins.

[4] I am learning the relationship between the specific plate boundaries and geologic features.

For Part 2 of this practice, write a series of learning intentions based on the standard and the learning progression presented. Remember, there will be many more steps in the learning progression.

STANDARD(S)

Understand the rule-making process in a direct democracy (everyone votes on the rules) and in a representative democracy (an elected group of people make the rules), giving examples of both systems in their classroom, school, and community. (Grade 1, CA Social Studies)

CONCEPTS (NOUNS)

Rule-making process
Direct democracy
Representative democracy
Key details

SKILLS (VERBS)

Understand
Give examples

LEARNING PROGRESSION

3. Compare and contrast direct and representative democracy.

LEARNING INTENTIONS

1. I am learning how direct democracy works through simulation.

2. I am learning how to identify examples of direct democracy in society.

3. I am learning how representative democracy works through simulation.

4. I am learning how to identify examples of representative democracy in society.

5. _____

6. _____

7. _____

8. _____

Module 4
Suggested Answers

For your first task in the Guided Practice section, consider the possible success criteria generated during a brainstorming session with teachers. Some of these are more appropriate than others. Which of them would be most appropriate? Which would not be as appropriate for the learning intention?

LEARNING INTENTION	SUCCESS CRITERIA	APPROPRIATE OR NOT
I am learning how to identify reliable and trustworthy content from the Internet.	I can use the "about" information to identify authority information.	Appropriate
	I can identify the date the information was published.	Not
	I can rate the accuracy of the information.	Appropriate
	I can use the domain name to identify credible sources (e.g., .com versus .edu or .gov).	Appropriate
	I can identify if the information is relevant to the research.	Not
I am learning how to recognize plants as the primary source of matter and energy entering most food chains.	I can compare plant and animal cells, noting differences in their structures.	Not
	I can define *source of matter* and *energy* as they related to food chains.	Appropriate
	I can analyze a food chain from a given biome and identify the role that plants play.	Appropriate
	I can identify producers and consumers in a food chain.	Appropriate
	I can name common plants that are included in the human food chain.	Appropriate (maybe)
I am learning how to demonstrate and explain how responses to music are informed by the context (such as social and cultural).	I can define the various ways people respond to music.	Appropriate
	I can explore the context of a given piece of music, including social, historical, and cultural influences.	Not
	I can identify personal preferences in music as informed by your own culture.	Appropriate
	I can describe the impact of context on audience reception of a given piece of music.	Appropriate
	I can explain how social and cultural influences shape popular music across time.	Not

For the second task, craft success criteria for each of the following learning intentions.

LEARNING INTENTION	SUCCESS CRITERIA
I am learning how to identify the impact of water pollution on the environment.	I can define types of water pollution.
	I can describe the effects of water pollution on water itself.
	I can describe the effects of water pollution on ecosystems.
I am learning how to describe how artists use tints and shades in painting.	I can describe how artists use tints and shades of color to express mood.
	I can describe how artists use tints and shades to portray dimension (depth and distance).
	I can describe how artists use tints and shades to illustrate motion.
I am learning how to partition shapes into parts with equal areas.	I can cut shapes and their partitions in half.
	I can cut shapes and their partitions into thirds.
	I can cut shapes and their partitions into fifths.
I am learning how to ask questions about unknown words in a text.	I can identify and note unknown words in a text.
	I can communicate the location of unknown words in a text to others.

Module 5
Suggested Answers

For your first task, consider the language learning expectations that follow and identify if they are more aligned with student needs in vocabulary, language structure, or language function.

EXAMPLES	V	S	F
Kindergarten: Language Arts **Content learning intention:** I am learning how to identify the important events after hearing a story. **Language learning intention:** I am learning how to retell the story and include at least three events.			x
Grade 1: Math **Content learning intention:** I am learning about how many tens and ones are in a set. **Language learning intention:** I am learning how to apply the sentence frame "___ sets of ten and ___ones equal ___." (Ex: "Three sets of tens and 2 ones equal 32.")		x	

EXAMPLES	V	S	F
Grade 2: Life Science **Content learning intention:** I am learning how to compare and contrast the life cycles. **Language learning intention:** I am learning how to summarize the similarities and differences between the life cycle of a frog and a butterfly.			x
Grade 3: Language Arts **Content learning intention:** I am learning how to evaluate key features of common texts. **Language learning intention:** I am learning how to justify why a passage is poetry, fiction, or nonfiction.			x
Grade 4: Earth Science **Content learning intention:** I am learning how to recognize how landslides, volcanic eruptions, and earthquakes cause changes to rocks. **Language learning intention:** Use technical vocabulary to discuss how rocks reflect the processes that formed them.	x		
Grade 5: Social Studies **Content learning intention:** I am learning how to analyze the major causes of the American Revolution. **Language learning intention:** I am learning how to apply compare/contrast signal words in a written explanation of the major causes of the American Revolution.		x	
Grade 6: Math **Content:** I am learning how to differentiate between relevant and irrelevant information in word problems. **Language learning intention:** I am learning how to explain which aspects of a word problem are relevant and irrelevant			x

V =Vocabulary (specialized, technical)

S = Language Structure (grammar, syntax, signal words, frames)

F = Language Function (instrumental, regulatory, interactional, personal, imaginative, heuristic, representational)

For the second task, modify each of the following learning intentions to include the language expectation identified.

LEARNING INTENTION	LANGUAGE EXPECTATION	MODIFIED VERSION OR LANGUAGE EXPECTATION
I am learning how to partition shapes into parts with equal areas.	Vocabulary	Correctly identify whether you are partitioning into halves, thirds, or fifths.
I am learning how to identify reliable and trustworthy content from the Internet.	Function	Explain why an Internet source is reliable and trustworthy.

(Continued)

LEARNING INTENTION	LANGUAGE EXPECTATION	MODIFIED VERSION OR LANGUAGE EXPECTATION
I am learning how to ask questions about unknown words in a text.	Structure	I found the unfamiliar word _____ in the sentence _____. I think it might mean _____ What does it mean?
I am learning how to identify the impact of water pollution on the environment.	Function	Describe how water pollution affects ecosystems.
I am learning how to demonstrate and explain how responses to music are informed by the context (such as social and cultural).	Vocabulary	Identify examples of social context and cultural context in discussion with peers.
I am learning how to describe how artists use tints and shades in painting.	Structure	Artists use _____ shades/tints in order to _____.
I am learning how to predict the geological features that result from specific plate boundaries (subduction zones, divergent margins, and transform margins).	Function	Justify your predictions by supporting them with evidence from your notes.

Module 6
Suggested Answers

For your first task, read each learning intentions and the potential talking points on relevance. Identify which of the talking points would be most effective for students to engage with the content.

LEARNING INTENTION	RELEVANCE	WHICH IS BETTER? WHY?
I am learning how to partition shapes into parts with equal areas.	1. You will need this on the upcoming test. 2. When we make fractional parts, we want to be fair and have each part the same size.	Number 2. It keeps the focus on growth and new learning not compliance. It foreshadows transfer to new learning to build relevance.
I am learning how to identify reliable and trustworthy content from the Internet.	1. Doing so makes sure that you are not a victim of crimes or lies. 2. If you know what is trustworthy you become a critical consumer of information.	Number 2. It actually encompasses Part 1, but goes more global. This provides more access points for relevance.

LEARNING INTENTION	RELEVANCE	WHICH IS BETTER? WHY?
I am learning how to ask questions about unknown words in a text.	1. Readers work to make meaning of the texts they read. 2. Asking questions helps you pay attention to what the author is saying. 3. When you find unknown words, you can add them to your vocabulary journal.	Number 1. This is the truth. This habit of mind will make students better readers and learners.
I am learning how to identify the impact of water pollution on the environment.	1. When you understand the causes and impact, you can help contribute to a healthy environment. 2. This unit will prepare you for the next one when we study the water cycle.	Number 1. This makes it personal and real, whereas the second one makes it about the class.
I am learning how to describe how artists use tints and shades in painting.	1. These are important words that you should know and be able to use on your own. 2. These concepts help you understand artistic style so that you can discuss art with others.	Number 2. It connects the learning to communication. The first one doesn't address why.
I am learning how to predict the geological features that result from a specific plate boundary (subduction zones, divergent margins, and transform margins).	1. This will help when you go to buy a house so that you are not buying near a dangerous area. 2. This is another opportunity for us to develop our predictive skills. 3. You will do better on the state test if you know this content.	Number 1 is narrow, but alluring. Number 2 is about transfer and useful habits of mind.

For your second task, review the learning intentions from the last unit and identify potential talking points for making these expectations relevant for students.

EXAMPLES	POTENTIAL TALKING POINTS ON RELEVANCE
Kindergarten: Language Arts **Content learning intention:** I am learning how to identify the important events after hearing a story. **Language learning intention:** I am learning how to retell the story and include at least three events.	· Knowing the important part of stories helps us remember them better.
Grade 1: Math **Content learning intention:** I am learning about how many tens and ones are in a set. **Language learning intention:** I am learning how to apply the sentence frame "___ sets of ten and ____ones equal ___." (Ex: "Three sets of ten and 2 ones equal 32.")	· Deconstructing numbers makes them easier to work with—especially when they get really big! · Thinking about numbers in this way is how algebra works, too!

EXAMPLES	POTENTIAL TALKING POINTS ON RELEVANCE
Grade 2: Life Science **Content learning intention:** I am learning how to compare and contrast the life cycles. **Language learning intention:** I am learning how to summarize the similarities and differences between the life cycle of a frog and a butterfly.	• Life is an amazing and diverse thing . . . you used to be babies and now you're children-soon you'll be adults! What if when you were babies you had tails? And what if when you became an adult you grew wings? In the life forms we will study today, that is exactly what happens!
Grade 3: Language Arts **Content learning intention:** I am learning how to evaluate key features of common texts. **Language learning intention:** I am learning how to justify why a passage is poetry, fiction, or nonfiction.	• Understanding the structure of a text helps us understand how it works and what it means.
Grade 4: Earth Science **Content learning intention:** I am learning how to recognize how landslides, volcanic eruptions, and earthquakes cause changes to rocks. **Language learning intention:** I am learning how to use technical vocabulary to discuss how rocks reflect the processes that formed them.	• Pick up any rock, anywhere. After today you will be able to tell exactly how that rock was formed, even if it happened millions of years ago!
Grade 5: Social Studies **Content learning intention:** I am learning how to analyze the major causes of the American Revolution. **Language learning intention:** I am learning how to apply compare/contrast signal words in a written explanation the major causes of the American Revolution.	• A lot of sacrifices were made so that we could become a country. We should know why. • Fairness and equity are things we are still working on as a country. And yet, they're why we are a country.
Grade 6: Math **Content:** I am learning how to differentiate between relevant and irrelevant information in word problems. **Language learning intention:** I am learning how to explain which aspects of a word problem are relevant and irrelevant.	• In real life, math typically isn't offered in nice, clean equations. It's up to us, the mathematicians, to change words and observations into equations so we can solve those problems.

Module 7
Suggested Answers

For your first task in this module, read each learning intention and the potential assessment opportunities that follow. Identify which of the assessments you believe would be most effective for students to engage with the content. In this case, there is no wrong answer. Select one of the two and identify why you believe it would be effective.

LEARNING INTENTION	ASSESSMENT OPPORTUNITY	WHICH ASSESSMENT? WHY?
I am learning how to partition shapes into parts with equal areas.	1. Use dry erase boards with partitioned shapes to hold up for peers and the teacher to check. 2. Use pattern blocks to demonstrate partitioning shapes equally.	1. Dry erase boards give students the freedom to design the shape and orientation of their partitions. Fraction shapes lift this load for them.
I am learning how to identify reliable and trustworthy content from the Internet.	1. Given a rubric and several websites, including fake websites (e.g., Pacific Northwest Octopus), students identify the reliability and trustworthiness of each. 2. Students analyze websites that they are using in their research, using the criteria for trustworthiness.	1. This method specifically targets the intended learning and provides iterated practice. Through this, the teacher can identify trends in misconceptions.
I am learning how to ask questions about unknown words in a text.	1. Discuss the words a student has circled in the text and the questions about the word that the student has written. 2. During a shared reading, students are invited to ask questions about words they do not know.	1. Method 2 requires students to speak up in order to be assessed. Method 1 allows the teacher to initiate these conversations—and even collect data pre-conversation via circled words.
I am learning how to identify the impact of water pollution on the environment.	1. Use a practice test to determine areas of mastery and areas of continued instructional need. 2. Summarize the impact in writing using targeted vocabulary and appropriate sentence frames.	1. Method 1 is a more holistic means of assessing all areas of mastery.
I am learning how to describe how artists use tints and shades in painting.	1. Listen in on partner conversations as students discuss the artists' choices. 2. Given a painting, students analyze the piece in writing, attending to tints and shades.	1. Listening to partner discussions allows real-time collection of data so the teacher can respond promptly.

(Continued)

LEARNING INTENTION	ASSESSMENT OPPORTUNITY	WHICH ASSESSMENT? WHY?
I am learning how to predict the geological features that result from specific plate boundaries (subduction zones, divergent margins, and transform margins).	1. After watching a video of a specific plate boundary, students predict the geological features before the video answers the question. 2. Use a practice test to determine areas of mastery and areas of continued instructional need.	1. This real-time assessment gives both the teacher and the student immediate feedback.

For your second task, review the learning intentions from the last unit and identify potential assessment opportunities for checking for understanding.

EXAMPLES	POTENTIAL ASSESSMENT OPPORTUNITIES
Kindergarten: Language Arts **Content learning intention:** I am learning how to identify the important events after hearing a story. **Language learning intention:** I am learning how to retell the story and include at least three events.	· Flipgrid retelling with three important events · Poll: Is ___ an important event?
Grade 1: Math **Content learning intention:** I am learning about how many tens and ones are in a set. **Language learning intention:** I am learning how to apply the sentence frame "___ sets of ten and ___ones equal ___." (Ex: "Three sets of ten and 2 ones equal 32.")	· Handheld whiteboard "show me" activity
Grade 2: Life Science **Content learning intention:** I am learning how to compare and contrast the life cycles. **Language learning intention:** I am learning how to summarize the similarities and differences between the life cycle of a frog and a butterfly.	· Interview table groups to check for understanding
Grade 3: Language Arts **Content learning intention:** I am learning how to evaluate key features of common texts. **Language learning intention:** I am learning how to justify why a passage is poetry, fiction, or nonfiction.	· Class poll: Is this passage poetry, fiction, or nonfiction? · Numbered heads to answer "why"
Grade 4: Earth Science **Content learning intention:** I am learning how to recognize how landslides, volcanic eruptions, and earthquakes cause changes to rocks. **Language learning intention:** I am learning how to use technical vocabulary to discuss how rocks reflect the processes that formed them.	· Exit tickets summarizing how specific rocks are formed

EXAMPLES	POTENTIAL ASSESSMENT OPPORTUNITIES
Grade 5: Social Studies **Content learning intention:** I am learning how to analyze the major causes of the American Revolution. **Language learning intention:** I am learning how to apply compare/contrast signal words in a written explanation of the major causes of the American Revolution.	· Draw a timeline of events leading up to the American Revolution on chart paper in groups
Grade 6: Math **Content:** I am learning how to differentiate between relevant and irrelevant information in word problems. **Language learning intention:** I am learning how to explain which aspects of a word problem are relevant and irrelevant.	· Exit tickets just asking students to cross out irrelevant info · Think Pair Poll: "Who thinks ___ is relevant?"

Module 8
Suggested Answers

For your first task, review each learning intention and the assessment opportunity. Describe how you could engage students in the targeted access point in the third column as part of a lesson. Of course, each lesson would have all access points, but we're just practicing here.

LEARNING INTENTION	ASSESSMENT OPPORTUNITY	MEANINGFUL INSTRUCTION
I am learning how to partition shapes into parts with equal areas.	Use pattern blocks to demonstrate partitioning shapes equally.	Collaborative: In table groups, students use fraction shapes to divide shapes into different partitions and record their work in drawings on a collaborative poster.
I am learning how to identify reliable and trustworthy content from the Internet.	Given a rubric and several websites, including fake websites (e.g., Pacific Northwest Octopus), students identify the reliability and trustworthiness of each.	Modeling: Think-Aloud: I know when I see a website ending in .edu, it is trustworthy because _____.
I am learning how to ask questions about unknown words in a text.	During a shared reading, students are invited to ask questions about words they do not know.	Modeling: As I read this passage, I realize I don't understand what the term *sole proprietor* means. So I'm circling it to tell myself to look it up or ask someone what it means when I reach the end.

LEARNING INTENTION	ASSESSMENT OPPORTUNITY	MEANINGFUL INSTRUCTION
I am learning how to identify the impact of water pollution on the environment.	Summarize the impact in writing using targeted vocabulary and appropriate sentence frames.	Independent: Write a summary describing the impact of water pollution using sentence frames if needed.
I am learning how to describe how artists use tints and shades in painting.	Listen in on partner conversations as students discuss the artists' choices.	Collaborative: Students compare and contrast various paintings in table groups with a focus on describing the use of tints and shades.
I am learning how to predict the geological features that result from specific plate boundaries (subduction zones, divergent margins, and transform margins).	After watching a video of a specific plate boundary, students predict the geological features before the video answers the question.	Guided: Pause the video before the reveal and facilitate discussions through questioning-prompting students toward the answers.

For your second task, revisit the previous learning intentions and identify one type of instruction required for students to master the learning intention. This could be focused instruction, guided instruction, collaborative learning opportunities, or independent learning.

EXAMPLES	IDEAS FOR MEANINGFUL INSTRUCTION
Kindergarten: Language Arts **Content learning intention:** I am learning how to identify the important events after hearing a story. **Language learning intention:** I am learning how to retell the story and include at least three events.	Modeling: Verbally annotate while reading a story. "I think this part is important because ____." Model retelling by focusing on important events.
Grade 1: Math **Content learning intention:** I am learning about how many tens and ones are in a set. **Language learning intention:** I am learning how to apply the sentence frame "___ sets of ten and ___ ones equal ___." (Ex: "Three sets of ten and 2 ones equal 32.")	Independent: Use the provided sentence frame along with base-ten blocks to solve problems from a problem set.
Grade 2: Life Science **Content learning intention:** I am learning how to compare and contrast the life cycles. **Language learning intention:** I am learning how to summarize the similarities and differences between the life cycle of a frog and a butterfly.	Collaborative: Collaborative poster with pre-printed cutouts of each animal's life cycle. Students work to design poster so that it compares, contrasts, and summarizes each life cycle.

EXAMPLES	IDEAS FOR MEANINGFUL INSTRUCTION
Grade 3: Language Arts **Content learning intention:** I am learning how to evaluate key features of common texts. **Language learning intention:** I am learning how to justify why a passage is poetry, fiction, or nonfiction.	Guided: What do we notice about the structure of the text? What details can help us decide whether it is poetry, fiction, or nonfiction? What kind of text is this?
Grade 4: Earth Science **Content learning intention:** I am learning how to recognize how landslides, volcanic eruptions, and earthquakes cause changes to rocks. **Language learning intention:** I am learning how to use technical vocabulary to discuss how rocks reflect the processes that formed them.	Collaborative: Students are paired and receive a rock sample (or picture) and have to prepare a mini-presentation (1 minute) in which they use technical vocabulary to describe how the rock was formed.
Grade 5: Social Studies **Content learning intention:** I am learning how to analyze the major causes of the American Revolution. **Language learning intention:** I am learning how to apply compare/contrast signal words in a written explanation the major causes of the American Revolution.	Independent: Write a three-paragraph essay comparing and contrasting two major causes of the American Revolution.
Grade 6: Math **Content:** I am learning how to differentiate between relevant and irrelevant information in word problems. **Language learning intention:** I am learning how to explain which aspects of a word problem are relevant and irrelevant.	Guided: What is the information in this line "_____"? Does this help us solve the problem? What is the problem asking for? Does this line "_____" help with that? Why or why not?

Module 9
Suggested Answers

For your first task, we have included a range of social studies and science standards. For each standard, we have identified ways that the standard might be assessed. Identify items for each that would allow teachers to determine student mastery of the content.

STANDARD	ASSESSMENT FORMAT	SAMPLE ITEMS OR TASKS FOR ASSESSMENT
Identify geographical features in their local region (e.g., deserts, mountains, valleys, hills, coastal areas, oceans, lakes). (Grade 3, CA)	Culminating group project	Group members gather pictures/video of local geography as part of a class presentation.

(Continued)

STANDARD	ASSESSMENT FORMAT	SAMPLE ITEMS OR TASKS FOR ASSESSMENT
Understand the relationship between religion and the social and political order in Mesopotamia and Egypt. (Grade 6, CA)	Multiple choice and dichotomous choice items	What was the type of religion in Mesopotamia? a. monotheistic b. polytheistic c. atheistic d. animism
Explain how the ideology of the France Revolution led France to develop from constitutional monarchy to democratic despotism to the Napoleonic empire. (Grade 10, CA)	Short, constructed response items	Explain why during the French Revolution France first developed from a constitutional monarchy to a democratic despotism.
Make observations to construct an evidence-based account that objects in darkness can be seen only when illuminated. (Grade 1, NCSS)	Culminating individual project	Record an "I can't see the . . ." video in which students display and explain the before-and-after effects of using a flashlight in the dark.
Identify evidence from patterns in rock formations and fossils in rock layers to support an explanation for changes in a landscape over time. (Grade 4, NGSS)	Performance	Given a picture of (an exaggerated) cross-section of rock layers, students write a short description of the landscape's history over time while citing evidence from the picture.
Construct and revise an explanation based on evidence for the cycling of matter and flow of energy in aerobic and anaerobic conditions. (HS, NGSS)	Extended essay response	Compare and contrast the role of aerobic and anaerobic respiration in two different environments. Discuss implications for living organisms and nonliving matter.

For your second task, review the assessment item and identify which aspects of relevancy the task could address. There may be more than one response for each.

ASSESSMENT ITEM	RELEVANCE CHECK
Complete the essay prompt and on a separate page identify the writing processes you used.	[x] Relevance outside the classroom [ ] Relevancy co-constructed with students [x] Relevance based on learning about oneself as a learner [x] Relevance within the discipline
We have the opportunity to recarpet the classroom, but we need to know the square footage of the room. How many different ways can you identify to figure out the size of the room?	[x] Relevance outside the classroom [ ] Relevancy co-constructed with students [ ] Relevance based on learning about oneself as a learner [x] Relevance within the discipline
This exam has five parts (multiple choice, true/false, matching, short responses, and fill in the blank). You should complete any two sections that allow you to demonstrate your understanding.	[ ] Relevance outside the classroom [x] Relevancy co-constructed with students [x] Relevance based on learning about oneself as a learner [ ] Relevance within the discipline
Generate 10 possible exam questions of any format. I will consider all of them as potential questions that allow the class to determine mastery of the content.	[ ] Relevance outside the classroom [x] Relevancy co-constructed with students [ ] Relevance based on learning about oneself as a learner [ ] Relevance within the discipline
Produce an iMovie in which you retell the content of this unit of study. You should have a narrator and include the technical vocabulary we have learned in this unit.	[x] Relevance outside the classroom [ ] Relevancy co-constructed with students [ ] Relevance based on learning about oneself as a learner [x] Relevance within the discipline

NOTES

REFERENCES

Cazden, C. B. (1988). *Classroom discourse: The language of teaching and learning*. Portsmouth, NH: Heinemann.

Davey, B. (1983). Thinking aloud—modeling the cognitive processes of reading comprehension. *Journal of Reading, 27*, 44–47.

DuFour, R., DuFour, R., Eaker, R., & Many, T. (2010). *Learning by doing: A handbook for professional learning communities at work*. Bloomington, IN: Solution Tree Press.

Fendick, F. (1990). *The correlation between teacher clarity of communication and student achievement gain: A meta-analysis*. Unpublished doctoral dissertation, University of Florida, Gainesville.

Fisher, D., & Frey, N. (2010). Unpacking the language purpose: Vocabulary, structure, and function. *TESOL Journal, 1*(3), 315–337.

Fisher, D., & Frey, N. (2014). *Better learning through structured teaching: A framework for the gradual release of responsibility* (2nd ed.). Alexandria, VA: ASCD.

Fisher, D., Frey, N., Almarode, J., Flories, K., & Nagel, D. (2019). *PLC+: Better decisions and greater impact by design*. Thousand Oaks, CA: Corwin.

Goddard, R. D., Hoy, W. K., & Hoy, A. W. (2000). Collective teacher efficacy: Its meaning, measure, and impact on student achievement. *American Educational Research Journal, 37*(2), 479–507.

Graff, G., & Birkenstein, C. (2013). *They say/I say: Academic moves that matter in academic writing*. New York, NY: W. W. Norton.

Hattie, J. (2009). *Visible learning: A synthesis of over 800 meta-analyses relating to achievement*. New York, NY: Routledge.

Hattie, J. (2012). *Visible learning for teachers: Maximizing impact on learning*. New York, NY: Routledge.

Hattie, J. A. C., & Donoghue, G. M. (2016). Learning strategies: A synthesis and conceptual model. *Science of Learning, 1*. doi:10.1038/npjscilearn2016

Lai, M., Wilson, A., McNaughton, S., & Hsiao, S. (2014). Improving achievement in secondary schools: Impact of a literacy project on reading comprehension and secondary school qualifications. *Reading Research Quarterly, 49*(3), 305–334.

Rubie-Davies, C., & Rosenthal, R. (2016). Intervening in teachers' expectations: A random effects meta-analytic approach to examining the effectiveness of an intervention. *Learning & Individual Differences, 50*, 83–92.

CORWIN
A SAGE Publishing Company

Helping educators make the greatest impact

CORWIN HAS ONE MISSION: to enhance education through intentional professional learning.

We build long-term relationships with our authors, educators, clients, and associations who partner with us to develop and continuously improve the best evidence-based practices that establish and support lifelong learning.